How Jesus Became God

Bart D. Ehrman, Ph.D.

THE
GREAT
COURSES°

PUBLISHED BY:

THE GREAT COURSES
Corporate Headquarters
4840 Westfields Boulevard, Suite 500
Chantilly, Virginia 20151-2299
Phone: 1-800-832-2412
Fax: 703-378-3819
www.thegreatcourses.com

Bart D. Ehrman, Ph.D.
James A. Gray Distinguished Professor
The University of North Carolina at Chapel Hill

Professor Bart D. Ehrman is the James A. Gray Distinguished Professor at The University of North Carolina (UNC) at Chapel Hill, where he has taught since 1988. He completed his undergraduate work at Wheaton College and received his M.Div. and Ph.D. from Princeton Theological Seminary. Before taking his position at UNC, Professor Ehrman taught at Rutgers University.

Professor Ehrman has published dozens of book reviews and scholarly articles for academic journals. He has written or edited 29 books, including 4 best sellers on *The New York Times* list: *Misquoting Jesus: The Story behind Who Changed the Bible and Why*; *God's Problem: How the Bible Fails to Answer Our Most Important Question—Why We Suffer*; *Jesus, Interrupted: Revealing the Hidden Contradictions in the Bible (and Why We Don't Know about Them)*; and *Forged: Writing in the Name of God—Why the Bible's Authors Are Not Who We Think They Are*.

Professor Ehrman also has served as president of the Society of Biblical Literature, Southeastern Region, and chair of the New Testament Textual Criticism Section of the society. His editorial positions have included associate editor for the *Journal of Early Christian Studies*, book review editor of the *Journal of Biblical Literature*, and editor of the Scholars' Press monograph series The New Testament in the Greek Fathers. He currently serves as coeditor of Brill's New Testament Tools, Studies and Documents series; coeditor in chief for *Vigiliae Christianae*, an international journal of early Christian studies; and area editor (early Christianity) for *The Encyclopedia of Ancient History*.

Professor Ehrman has received several teaching awards, including the John William Pope Center Spirit of Inquiry Award, the UNC Students' Undergraduate Teaching Award, the Phillip and Ruth Hettleman Prize for

Artistic and Scholarly Achievement by Young Faculty, the Bowman and Gordon Gray Professorship (awarded for excellence in undergraduate teaching), and the Religious Liberty Award from the American Humanist Association.

Professor Ehrman has been featured widely in television, radio, and print media, including *The Daily Show with Jon Stewart*, *The Colbert Report*, CNN, Discovery Channel, HISTORY, *National Geographic*, BBC, *Fresh Air*, *Talk of the Nation*, *TIME*, *Newsweek*, *The New York Times*, and *The Washington Post*.

For The Great Courses, Professor Ehrman has taught *The Greatest Controversies of Early Christian History*; *The New Testament*; *The History of the Bible: The Making of the New Testament Canon*; *Lost Christianities: Christian Scriptures and the Battles over Authentication*; *From Jesus to Constantine: A History of Early Christianity*; *The Historical Jesus*; and *After the New Testament: The Writings of the Apostolic Fathers*. ■

Table of Contents

Table of Contents

Table of Contents

How Jesus Became God

Scope:

Jesus of Nazareth was a preacher of the imminent apocalypse, who proclaimed that God was soon going to intervene in history, overthrow the forces of evil, and set up a good kingdom here on earth. In the last week of his life, Jesus took his message to Jerusalem, the capital city of Judea, and there, faced violent opposition. He was arrested, put on trial, charged with imagining himself the future king of the Jews, and condemned to death by crucifixion. He died as a powerless and forsaken Jewish preacher of an apocalypse that never came.

Yet four centuries later, millions of people throughout the Roman Empire considered Jesus not to be a failed Jewish prophet but to be a divine being, none other than the God who created the universe, equal in power and stature with God the Father Almighty.

This course addresses the question of how that happened. How did the rejected Jewish preacher who ended up on the wrong side of the law and was crucified for his efforts come to be thought of as the Lord and creator of all things, a member of the divine Trinity? How did Jesus become God?

The course begins by situating this transformation of Jesus from Jewish preacher to Lord God within its historical context, by examining how ancient people more broadly understood that gods could become human and humans could become gods. In two lectures, we see that this was a common theme of ancient Greek and Roman mythology and popular thought; in two additional lectures, we see how even within Judaism, it was thought that there could be human divinities, on one hand, and divine humans, on the other.

From there, we move to the life of the historical Jesus to see the focal points of his ministry and, especially, to ask whether he considered himself divine. It is true that in the final Gospel of the New Testament—the Gospel of John—Jesus is called and understood to be God, and of course, throughout history, Christians have maintained that this is what Jesus said about himself. But is that historically accurate? We will see reasons that historians and biblical scholars have adduced for thinking that this was not, in fact, an element of Jesus's public message.

In the following lectures, we will look at the key event that promoted the idea that Jesus was God, despite what his followers thought about him during his lifetime. We will see why it was the belief in Jesus's Resurrection that led his disciples to think he had been elevated to a divine position in heaven and, at that point, "made" into a divine being. In the course of our deliberations, we will consider what historians can say about Jesus's death and Resurrection: Was he actually buried in a known tomb? Was the tomb discovered to be empty three days later? Did his disciples have visions of Jesus after his death? In particular, we will see why belief in the Resurrection not only marks the beginning of the Christian religion but also—and closely related—started the belief that Jesus had been made God.

Over time, Christians who originally thought Jesus had become a divine being at the Resurrection came to think that, instead, he had been adopted to be divine at his baptism (as in the Gospel of Mark) or that he had been born as the Son of God (as in Matthew and Luke). Eventually, Christians moved beyond the idea that Jesus had become the Son of God to the notion that he had been God before coming into the world, a view we find in the writings of the apostle Paul and in the Gospel of John.

After completing this survey of views of Jesus's divinity within the pages of the New Testament, we move to the 2nd and 3rd centuries, when Christians of different theological persuasions had a variety of ways to understand how Christ could be God. Here we consider docetic understandings of Christ, according to which he was so much God that he had never actually been human; Gnostic understandings that the man Jesus was a different being from the divine Christ, who was a God who temporarily inhabited Jesus's body during his public ministry; and modalist understandings, according to which Jesus was God because he was none other than God the Father appearing in the flesh.

In following lectures, we will see that debates over these issues are what led to the Christian doctrine of the Trinity, that there are three persons, all of whom are God—Father, Son, and Holy Spirit—but that even though there are three of them, there is only one God. This discussion will take us up to the last portion of the course, a look at the Arian controversy that divided the Christian church in the 4th century. This conflict centered on a theologian named Arius who argued that Jesus was a secondary, subordinate divinity who had been created before the universe by God the Father. Arius was attacked by others who said that Christ had always existed—he had never come into being—and rather than being subordinate to God the Father, he was fully equal with him.

In the final lectures, we will see that the Roman emperor Constantine—the first emperor to convert to the Christian faith—called the Council of Nicea to resolve this dispute between Arius and his opponents. Arius was defeated, and Christ was proclaimed coeternal and completely equal with God the Father. Even so, as we will see, the controversies and their implications continued on into the centuries that followed.

The entire story of how Jesus became God is of paramount importance not only to those interested in the Christian religion for personal or historical reasons but also for everyone who has the slightest interest in history. If Jesus had not been declared God at his Resurrection, his followers would have remained a small sect within Judaism whose leader ended up on the wrong side of the law and was crucified for his efforts. The massive conversion of Gentiles to belief in Christ would never have happened. Centuries later, the Roman emperor would never have converted. The Roman Empire would never have adopted Christian beliefs and ways. The Middle Ages, the Renaissance, the Reformation, and modernity as we know it would never have transpired. And most of us would still be pagan. It is for this reason that there are indeed few questions in the entire history of civilization as important as this one: How did Jesus become God? ■

Jesus—The Man Who Became God

Lecture 1

Of course, there are enormous differences in belief among various Christian denominations, but all Christian groups agree on one thing: Jesus was not a mere human but was himself God. This religious/theological view differs from scholarly views, which also offer a variety of perspectives on the historical Jesus. Still, scholars share the recognition that Jesus was not considered to be more than a man during his lifetime. Somehow, he ended up on the wrong side of the law, was condemned for treason, and was crucified. Those facts return us to our central question: How did a Jewish preacher executed for crimes against the state come to be seen as the Lord God Almighty? How did Jesus become God?

A Crucial Question

- The question of how Jesus became God may seem on the surface to be a matter of theological interest only, important only to Christian believers and scholars. But in fact, it is a question that should matter to everyone who thinks that history matters, whether Christian or not. As we will see in this course, it is among the most significant historical questions in all of Western civilization.

- If Jesus had never come to be considered God, Western civilization as we know it would never have developed. To explain why this is so requires a good bit of background.
  - Whatever else the historical Jesus may have been, Jesus of Nazareth was a Jewish preacher who proclaimed that God's kingdom was soon to come to earth.

  - Jesus's followers were lower-class, Aramaic-speaking peasants from Galilee. During his ministry, they had no sense that he was planning to start a new religion. In their view, he was giving them the true and correct understanding of their own religion, Judaism.

o   As we will see at length in this course, those followers had no inkling during his lifetime that Jesus was anything other than human. It was only after his death that many of them came to believe that he had been raised from the dead and exalted to the divine realm; for them, in some way and in some sense, this made Jesus into a divine being.

o   That is what led them to develop a new religion—not the Jewish religion they had while they followed Jesus on earth but a Christian religion predicated on the idea that Jesus was a divine being who had died and had been raised from the dead.

o   If Jesus had never come to be considered God, his followers would have remained within their Jewish communities as Jews who thought their now-dead teacher was the one who gave them true insights into what the religion both was and was supposed to be. In other words, the followers of Jesus would have remained a sect within Judaism.

o   But because they began to think that Jesus was more than human, their message began to appeal to outsiders. Missionaries, such as Paul, began to insist that a person did not have to be a Jew to be a follower of Jesus. Non-Jews began to convert more often than Jews to this new faith.

o   These non-Jews in particular would have had no problem believing that a human could also be divine, and their faith in this divine man Jesus began to spread rapidly throughout the Roman world. Through evangelism and missionary work, Christianity gradually grew at a rate of about 40 percent every decade. By the beginning of the 4th century, nearly 5 percent of the empire was Christian.

o   When the emperor Constantine converted to the faith, Christianity changed from being a persecuted, marginalized religion to becoming the dominant religious force in the empire. With imperial backing, it could also consolidate itself and utilize secular power to enforce its theological beliefs, including the belief that Jesus himself was God.

o What all this means is that if the followers of Jesus had never decided that he was not a mere mortal, the Christian religion would have remained a part of Judaism, and

The conversion of the emperor Constantine to Christianity in the early 4th century transformed the faith into the dominant religious force in the Roman Empire.

the Roman Empire would never have been taken over by the religion. As a result, the history of late antiquity, the Middle Ages, the Renaissance, the Reformation, and modernity as we know it would never have transpired.

o Thus, the early Christian claim that Jesus was himself God completely altered the course of world history for all time.

Jesus as God in Modern Times
- The fact that Jesus's followers began to call him God affects not only the history of Western civilization but also billions of lives in our own day.

- In our world today, some two billion people consider themselves to be Christian. The vast majority of these two billion people believe that Jesus is, in some sense, God.

- The Christian religion affects not only what people believe but also how they choose to live their lives, what ethical choices they make, how they engage in politics, what economic theories they support, and what social structures they believe in.

- If Jesus were thought to be merely another human, many of these Christians—arguably most—would not have their Christian faith to help guide their beliefs, ethics, and social and political views.

- This is less a question of who Jesus really was than who he was—and continues to be—perceived to be by his followers.

Timeline and Overview of Early Christian Belief
- We are not completely certain about Jesus's dates. The usual date of his birth is given as 4 B.C.E. because that is when King Herod died. Jesus probably died around 30 C.E., under Pilate, who ruled from 26 to 36 C.E.

- Our first Christian author was Paul, writing around 50 to 60 C.E. The New Testament Gospels were probably written between 65 and 95 C.E., with Mark first, then Matthew and Luke, and then John.

- Probably during the period of the New Testament—the first century of the Christian faith—there were many different views about Jesus, God, salvation, and other issues.
  - It has proved difficult for historians to establish what different communities of Christians believed in this earliest period of the church, in no small measure because we are so restricted in our surviving sources of information.

  - Still, Paul's views differed from those of his opponents in Galatia and Corinth, including their views of the significance of Jesus's death and Resurrection.

- This early diversity becomes clearer in later periods. Already in the 2nd and 3rd centuries, Christianity was astonishingly diversified, with Christian leaders and their congregations disagreeing on absolutely fundamental issues.

- o This can be seen in ancient Christian views of God—whether the God of the Bible was good or evil.

- o We also find disagreement in views of creation—whether the world was the good creation of a loving God or an evil place manufactured by ignorant and wicked divinities.

- o And we see disagreement in views of Scripture—whether the Jewish Bible was a revelation from on high or a book meant to lead the human race astray.

- These ancient differences attested in the 2nd and 3rd centuries were especially evident in Christian understandings of Jesus.
  - o Was he a man but not God?

  - o Was he God but not a man?

  - o Was he two different beings, one a god and the other a man?

  - o Was he one being, partially God and partially man?

  - o Was he one being, fully God and fully man? If so, how was that possible?

The Nicene Creed
- The debates over who Christ really was came to culmination in the early 4th century, soon after the conversion of Constantine.

- Starting in the early 4th century, leaders of the church began to hold conferences at which they could hammer out statements of faith to be subscribed to by all believers.

- Christian creeds began to be written: statements of faith to be adhered to by all those who confessed themselves to be Christian.

- The most famous of these is the Nicene Creed, so-called because it was adopted by a council of bishops of the church from around the world, who gathered to debate these issues in Nicaea, a city in Asia Minor (modern Turkey).

- The Nicene Creed is clear and definitive in its affirmation that Christ is God. He is not the same as God the Father, but he is equal with him in every way and not at all subordinate to him. He always existed, and he was the one who created the universe.

- This became the standard belief in the Christian church and, eventually, the standard belief of the Roman emperors themselves.

- If Jesus had remained a crucified Jew—and not God—Christianity would never have become the religion of Rome; we would not have had the history of the West; and countless people would probably have remained pagan.

Course Overview
- Throughout these 24 lectures, we will go into considerable depth on a number of important questions.

- How did ancient peoples—both pagans and Jews—understand that gods could become humans and humans could be gods?

- What were the main characteristics of Jesus's public ministry and proclamation? In particular, what did he teach and say about himself?

- What exactly made the first Christians say that Jesus was more than a Jewish teacher?

- When did the early Christians first declare that Jesus was God, and what did they mean by that declaration at first?

- How did early Christians debate the nature of Christ in the following centuries?

- And how did the 4th-century sense, which has been handed down to Christians today, emerge out of those debates, so that Jesus was not only divine in some sense, but he was fully God, creator of heaven and earth?

Suggested Reading

Ehrman, *How Jesus Became God: The Exaltation of a Jewish Preacher from Galilee.*

Questions to Consider

1. Think of as many different views of Jesus found among Christians you know about in the world today. What, if anything, do they all have in common?

2. Try to think of all the ways our world would be different if Christianity had not become the dominant religion of the West some three or four centuries after Jesus lived.

Greco-Roman Gods Who Became Human
Lecture 2

The ancient world knew of more than one mortal who was thought to be the Son of God, such as the pagan philosopher Apollonius of Tyana, said to have performed miracles and to have ascended to heaven at his death. How could ancient people believe that a human could be a god or a god could be a human? To answer this question, we need to know more about religion in the Greco-Roman world.

Apollonius of Tyana
- About 2,000 years ago, a remarkable man was born in a remote part of the Roman Empire. His mother was told that he would not be a mortal but, in fact, would be divine. She gave birth to him in a miraculous way.

- As an adult, this man collected disciples around him who came to believe that he was the Son of God. And he did miracles to prove his divinity—healing the sick, casting out demons, and raising the dead. At the end of his life, he ascended to heaven.

- This man was Apollonius of Tyana, a pagan philosopher active some 50 years after Jesus and widely known in his own day.

- We know about the life of Apollonius from the writings of his later follower Philostratus, who based his account, he tells us, on earlier eyewitness reports.

- Later, there were debates between the followers of Jesus and the followers of Apollonius, concerning which was the Son of God and which was a fraud. We see these debates in a battle of words between the pagan Hierocles and the Christian Eusebius.

- But it is important to note that these were not the only two miracle-working Sons of God in the ancient world. There were, in fact, a number of them—enough so that the idea of a divine human being was widely known throughout antiquity.

- To understand how ancient people could believe that a human could be a god or a god could be a human, we need to know more about religion in the Greco-Roman world.

Ancient Polytheism
- Virtually everyone in the ancient world was a polytheist—apart from Jews and, eventually, Christians. Scholars sometimes call these Greco-Roman religions "pagan," which in this context does not have a derogatory connotation.

- Greek and Roman polytheists had thousands of different religions, but they had numerous features in common.
  o These polytheistic religions had many gods—gods of every function, purpose, and place imaginable.

  o These gods were to be worshipped by prayers and sacrifices.

  o Such worship pleased the gods, and in return, they could help humans through the difficulties of life.

- Polytheist religions did not maintain that there was a vast chasm that separated the divine from the human realms.
  o This is the common conception today, especially in the Western religions (Judaism, Christianity, and Islam), but it was not a widely held view in antiquity.

  o For ancient Greeks and Romans, the divine realm and the human realms were heavily populated, and both humans and divinities were on a kind of continuum of magnificence and power.

  o The two continua sometimes overlapped; thus, gods could be, in some sense, human, and some humans could be, in some sense, divine.

- It may be easiest to imagine the divine realm for ancient pagans as a kind of pyramid, with the very top spot occupied by the one ultimate god; the next tier, by the great gods of Greece and Rome; the next, by local and less powerful divinities; the next, by *daimonia* (spirit beings less powerful than the gods but more directly involved in human affairs); and the final tier occupied by "divine humans."
  o Below that tier were the humans, who themselves could be ranked in terms of their power, intelligence, and beauty.

  o In this understanding, there is not a chasm separating the divine and human realms but a kind of continuity.

Models of Divine Men
- In this ancient view of the divine realm, gods could sometimes be or become humans, and humans could sometimes be or become gods. There were three basic models for "divine men" in this world.

- Sometimes it was understood that gods could and would come down to earth in human form to make a temporary visit for purposes of their own.

- Sometimes it was understood that a person was born from the sexual union of a god and a mortal; thus, that the person was, in some sense, part divine and part human.

- Sometimes it was understood that a human was elevated by the gods to their realm, usually after death, and at that point divinized, made into a god.

Gods Becoming Human
- There are numerous stories in the ancient myths about gods temporarily assuming human form to meet, speak, and interact with humans.

- These stories in many ways are similar to later Christian beliefs about Christ being a preexistent divine being who came to earth as a human, only later to return to the heavenly realm.

- The pagan stories, of course, can be found in ancient Greek and Roman mythology. One interesting example that serves to illustrate the point is the account told by the Roman author Ovid of the temporary "incarnation" of Jupiter and Mercury and their meeting with the poor elderly couple Philemon and Baucis.
  - *Incarnation* literally means "coming in the flesh." The gods sometimes did that, according to the mythical tales related by Ovid.

  - Ovid was one of the great authors of Roman antiquity, who narrated stories that had been passed down for centuries, especially in his book *Metamorphoses*.

  - In the story we are interested in, Jupiter, the chief god, and Mercury, the messenger of the gods, temporarily took on human form and visited a region of Asia Minor. Only Philemon and Baucis, a sweet elderly couple, welcomed the gods into their home.

  - As a result, even though everyone who had rejected the gods was to be destroyed, these two were given any wish they desired. They asked to be made head of the gods' shrine and to die in unison.

  - Here, we have a tale of gods who visit humans, in human form, for a relatively short time. They are indistinguishable from other humans; they interact with humans; and their interactions bring both judgment and blessing.

Ovid's Story and the New Testament
- The story of Jupiter and Mercury appears to lie behind an interesting account found in the New Testament, in the book of Acts, an account of the missionary activities of Jesus's followers after his death

- Traveling in the same region of Asia Minor, the apostles Paul and Barnabas are mistaken, by a miracle they perform, as Zeus and Hermes. (Zeus was the Greek version of the Roman Jupiter; Hermes, the Greek version of Mercury.) The people in this region remembered the story of Philemon and Baucis and did not want to replicate the mistake of those who were judged by the gods.

• These two stories show one of the ways that ancient people imagined how something like divine men could exist: Gods could assume, temporarily, the guise of humans in order to visit people and interact with them.

The ancient understanding of the divine realm encompassed a kind of continuity with the human realm, rather than a chasm separating the two.

Suggested Reading

Cartlidge and Dungan, eds., *Documents for the Study of the Gospels*.

Ehrman, *How Jesus Became God: The Exaltation of a Jewish Preacher from Galilee*.

Hengel, *The Son of God*.

Lane Fox, *Pagans and Christians*.

Peppard, *The Son of God in the Roman World*.

Rives, *Religion in the Roman Empire*.

Turcan, *The Cults of the Roman Empire*.

Questions to Consider

1. What are the most significant ways that the religions of ancient pagans differed from religion as we know it today?

2. In what ways is the idea of Christ becoming human both like and unlike pagan myths about other gods becoming human?

Humans as Gods in the Greco-Roman World
Lecture 3

A s we've seen, the vast majority of the inhabitants of the Greco-Roman world were polytheists. They did not believe that there was a great chasm between the divine and human realms but understood that these realms could overlap. We have looked at one model of this overlap: divine beings becoming human. In this lecture, we will look at two other models: humans born to gods and humans who were exalted to heaven, usually at death, to become one of the gods.

Humans Born of the Gods
- In the ancient world, it was not uncommon for an exceedingly powerful or intelligent person to be thought of as more than human.

- In some cases that status was because he was not, in fact, a mere mortal but had one of the gods as his father. This was the case with Alexander the Great, rumored to be the son of Zeus.
  - A humorous account of such a birth is told by the Roman playwright Plautus in his work *Amphitryon*. Here, Alcmena, the mother of Hercules, is made pregnant by Zeus's Roman counterpart, Jupiter. The god disguises himself to resemble Alcmena's husband, Amphitryon, in order to spend a long night frolicking in her arms.

  - It is not clear that anyone actually believed that this story was history, but it was seen as a plausible view: Sometimes gods had sex with women, and the result was a demigod, part god and part human.

Apotheosis
- A third way a human could also be or become divine involves a process known as *apotheosis*—the act by which a human is made into a god. We have seen an instance of this already in Ovid's story of the elderly couple Philemon and Baucis.

17

- More commonly this divinization of a human involved great philosophers or, more commonly still, incredibly powerful rulers.
  - The Roman historian Livy tells of how Romulus, the founder and first king of Rome, was thought to have been taken up to the divine realm as a god at the end of his life.

  - The Roman biographer Suetonius discusses the idea that Julius Caesar was thought to have been made a god after he died.

  - In Caesar's case, it is not surprising that his adopted son, Octavian (who was later to become Caesar Augustus, the first Roman emperor), encouraged the belief that his father had become a god. If his father was a god, what did that make Octavian?

The Cult of the Emperor
- With Caesar Augustus, we have the beginning of the emperor cult, the practice of honoring emperors, both dead and living, as gods. Note that the word *cult* is not derogatory in this context but refers to the care of the gods.

- In Greece, Alexander the Great—300 years before Octavian—accepted divine honors, allowing his subjects to make sacrifices to him. Roman emperors were also accorded such honors, otherwise reserved for the gods.

- Thus, the Roman orator Quintilian speaks of gods who were born divine and of other gods who had "won immortality by their valor," that is, those who had been made gods because of their amazing deeds.

- In the Roman world, this normally happened after an emperor had died, based on a vote of the Senate, seen to ratify an emperor's divine status.

- But it often happened for living emperors, as well, as can be seen, for example, in an inscription from Pergamum dedicated to the god Augustus Caesar or one in Miletus dedicated to the emperor Caligula, who is called the god Sebastos.

- How are we to understand this adoration of the emperor as a divine being?

In other ancient societies, such as Egypt, it was thought that the ruler—the pharaoh—was an embodiment of a god.

  o The older view of scholarship was that we should not take it seriously. In this view, those said to be gods were known to be as human as anyone else. The emperor cult was simply political propaganda, which no one ever really believed, that encouraged people to worship their leaders as divine. Logically, if the ruler is divine, then he cannot be disobeyed.

  o Recent scholarship has reevaluated this older view and offered a different perspective. There is little evidence that the worship of the emperor was promoted by the officials of Rome itself and rarely by the emperors. These were grassroots movements, in which rulers were revered for their superhuman power and authority.

  o Whether or not people actually believed in their hearts that the emperors were gods is impossible to know. However, the emperors were certainly treated as gods, for example, by having sacrifices performed not only on their behalf but also to them and by having temples built and dedicated to them.

- Like the gods, the emperors could provide enormous benefits to their people; thus, they had divine-like power. And as we have seen, they, too, could be called god.

- This adoration of divine rulers was not restricted to Rome. It can be seen clearly in an inscription dedicated to the ruler of Syria, Antiochus, and his wife Laodice in gratitude for their overcoming a foreign power. The city Teas set up cult statues of the two, performed sacrifices at a public ceremony, and honored them with an inscription in which they were placed on the same level as the local god Dionysus and said to be "common saviors of our city."

Divine Humans

- In short, Jesus was not the only divine man in the ancient world.
  - Some were thought to have been gods who came down to earth temporarily in human form.

  - Others were thought to have been literally the son of a god, the divine product of the union of a god and a mortal woman.

  - Still others were thought to have been taken up into heaven at the end of their lives to live and rule in the divine realm.

- Jesus, as we will see, was thought to be all three of these things by different Christians in different times and different places.

Suggested Reading

Cartlidge and Dungan, eds., *Documents for the Study of the Gospels*.

Ehrman, *How Jesus Became God: The Exaltation of a Jewish Preacher from Galilee*.

Friesen, *Imperial Cults and the Apocalypse of John*.

Hengel, *The Son of God*.

Lane Fox, *Pagans and Christians*.

Peppard, *The Son of God in the Roman World*.

Price, *Rituals and Power*.

Rives, *Religion in the Roman Empire*.

Turcan, *The Cults of the Roman Empire*.

Questions to Consider

1. In what ways are the stories of Jesus's virgin birth like and unlike Greek and Roman myths about people born to the union of a god and a mortal?

2. In what ways would Jesus have been seen as similar and dissimilar to that other "Son of God" in the ancient world, the Roman emperor?

Gods Who Were Human in Ancient Judaism
Lecture 4

To this point in our course, we have discussed the pagans of the Roman Empire, that is, the polytheists who believed in many gods and who made up about 93 percent of the empire. Even if these people understood that there was a kind of divine pyramid with a range of more or less powerful gods and that gods could become human and humans could become gods, what does that have to do with Jesus and Christianity? In this lecture, we'll see that even within Judaism, there was a widespread belief that divine beings could become human temporarily and that they had, in fact, done so on a number of occasions. In this belief, Jews were not all that different from their pagan neighbors.

Divine Beings in Ancient Judaism

- It is true that Judaism was distinctive among all the religions of the Greco-Roman world in insisting that only one God was the true divinity worthy of worship. In fact, by the time of Jesus, most Jews were monotheists, believing that there was only one God and that the gods of the pagans did not actually exist.

- But it had not always been that way in Judaism. For centuries, many Israelites were not monotheists but henotheists; they believed that other gods existed, but they were not to be worshipped, as evidenced already in the Ten Commandments.

- Eventually, a strain of monotheism developed within ancient Israel, as evident in such passages of the Hebrew Bible as Isaiah 45.

- If that was the case in the days of Jesus, is it true, then, that there could be no other divine beings who interacted with humans? Was there just God in heaven and we mortals on earth?

- In point of fact, even Jews who were monotheists still believed in other divine beings, that is, hyper-intelligent beings who were superhuman; who lived in the divine realm, not here on earth; and who were far more powerful than mere mortals. Among these beings were angels, archangels, cherubim, and seraphim—all mentioned in the Bible.

Divine Beings as God

- Sometimes, the Bible speaks of one of these other divine beings coming to earth in the shape of a human, and sometimes, these other divine beings who appear as humans are actually called God or identified as the Lord God himself. Sometimes, God himself appears on earth in human or other form.

- Already in the book of Genesis, the father of Israel, Abraham, is said to have an encounter with three "men." Later in the story, two of these men are revealed to be angels, and the third is God.

In Exodus 3, God appears as a burning bush, commanding Moses to bring the Israelites out of Egypt.

23

- The most famous instance of an angel being identified as God occurs in Exodus 3 at the burning bush. Here, Moses is addressed by the "Angel of the Lord," who is then later called "the Lord."

- This Angel of the Lord also sometimes appears to humans as himself a human. We see an example in Genesis 16, when the Angel of the Lord speaks with and rescues a woman named Hagar from near death from exposure.

- In other passages of the Bible, we are told that angels are either sons of God or God himself and that they become human.
  - This is implied in the famous passage in Job 1, when the "sons of God" appear before God in his divine council.

  - Angels are explicitly called gods in Psalm 82.

  - In other Jewish traditions, angels are said to become human, as in the text known as the Prayer of Joseph.

- In addition, and equally striking, we are told in some Jewish texts that humans can become angels. This is clearly laid out in 2 Baruch 51 and 2 Enoch 22.

- In sum, in the Jewish tradition, there are divine beings other than God who are called gods; these divine beings can become human; God himself sometimes appears temporarily in human form; and humans themselves can sometimes become angelic beings.

Beings Born of Divine Union

- Moreover, we also have stories in the Jewish tradition of beings who are born to the union of divinities and humans.

- This is the point of the bizarre passage in Genesis 6, where the "sons of God" take wives among the "daughters of men" and produce semi-divine offspring. This story is expounded in the book of 1 Enoch, a later Jewish text that understood the offspring to be malevolent giants.

- The idea that other beings besides the one true God could be called gods is found not only in the pagan but also in the Jewish tradition, and just as pagans thought gods could temporarily become human and that some people were born to the union of divine and human beings, so, too, did many Jews in the days of Jesus.

Suggested Reading

Cartlidge and Dungan, eds., *Documents for the Study of the Gospels*.

Ehrman, *How Jesus Became God: The Exaltation of a Jewish Preacher from Galilee*.

Fredriksen, *From Jesus to Christ*.

Garrett, *No Ordinary Angel*.

Gieschen, *Angelomorphic Christology*.

Hengel, *The Son of God*.

Hurtado, *Lord Jesus Christ*.

———, *One God, One Lord*.

Sanders, *Judaism Practice and Belief, 63 BCE–66 CE*.

Questions to Consider

1. In what ways was Judaism in antiquity different from the pagan religions of Rome and Greece?

2. How are the Jewish stories of divine beings becoming human like and unlike such stories in Greek and Roman sources?

Ancient Jews Who Were Gods

Lecture 5

We have seen that Jews, like pagans, understood that the divine realm was populated with superhuman beings besides the Lord God Almighty, that sometimes these divine beings were called gods, and sometimes these other gods—or even the one God himself—would appear on earth as humans. In this lecture, we will see that the reverse was true, as well: Even among Jews, it was believed that humans could be made into divine beings and that sometimes men were actually called God.

The Son of Man

- One of the most interesting divine figures in ancient Judaism was known as "the Son of Man."

- We first encounter some version of this figure in the bizarre vision of Daniel 7. Here, the prophet experiences a night vision, in which he sees four terrible beasts that emerge out of the sea and wreak havoc on the earth, destroying peoples and kingdoms. Then, "one like a Son of Man" arrives from heaven, to whom is given all authority and power forever.

- In Daniel's vision, this "one like a Son of Man" is probably to be understood as the nation Israel itself. Eventually, it came to be thought of as an angelic being, an individual sent from heaven as the judge of earth.

- We see this understanding in a later Jewish text called 1 Enoch, written probably some years before the New Testament. In a section of 1 Enoch known as the Similitudes, we find an extensive set of reflections on the Son of Man, who actually sits on God's throne and is called the judge of the earth.

- There were other figures who were thought to have shared the throne of God in heaven as a kind of second God; the rabbis of later times talk about Jews who hold such views, in which some kind of angelic being rules the world along with God.

o Some texts speak about the "two powers in heaven"; this second divine being is placed on a level with God himself.

o This idea is sometimes cited to explain who God is speaking to in Genesis 1:26, when he creates humans by saying: "Let us make man in our own image."

- In addition, some Jews considered divine attributes of God to be divine beings apart from God. The word scholars use for these divinized attributes of God is *hypostases*.

o The basic idea here is that certain characteristics of God could exist apart from him, but because they are his own characteristics, they are, like him, divine.

o The fact that God is wise means that he has wisdom. But because wisdom is something God "has," then it is something that also exists apart from him. And because it is God's wisdom, it is divine.

o Thus, one of the hypostases that some ancient Jews considered to be a god was Wisdom, as based, for example, on Proverbs 8.

o Sometimes God's "Word" was also thought to be divine, as based on Genesis 1 and as seen in the explanations of the great Jewish philosopher of the 1st century C.E., Philo, who thought that the Word existed apart from God but also was God.

Human Beings as God

- In addition to all these other divine entities being thought of as God, Jewish texts—even in the Bible—sometimes refer to human beings as God. This is true, for example, of Moses.

o In the book of Exodus, Moses is said to have functioned as "God" for his brother Aaron (Exodus 4:16).

- o In the writings of Philo, Moses is not only called the most perfect man that ever lived, but he is said to have had a divine intellect, to have gradually become divine over the course of his life, and at the end, to have been "called the god and king of the entire nation."

- • Just as striking, sometimes the king of Israel was called God.
  - o The roots of this view are in the promise to David in 2 Samuel 7:13–16 that his son would also be a Son of God.

  - o We have seen that rulers in Egypt were thought of as divine beings; the same thing was true in some parts of Israel.

  - o This is the intimation of Psalm 2:7; the king is "begotten" to be the Son of God.

  - o And more than that, the king is explicitly called "God" in Isaiah 45 and Isaiah 9.

- • In none of these instances is Moses, or the king of Israel, or even the Son of Man or Wisdom or the Word thought to be the Lord God Almighty himself. They are always a second being who is considered to be God along with the Lord God.
  - o This is the matrix within which Jesus lived and died and within which Christianity developed.

  - o Christians—very soon after Jesus died—began calling him God. That did not mean he was the Lord God Almighty, but he was still, in some sense, God. There was a solid precedent for this view not just among the polytheistic religions of the time but also within Judaism.

Suggested Reading

Ehrman, *How Jesus Became God: The Exaltation of a Jewish Preacher from Galilee.*

Fredriksen, *From Jesus to Christ.*

Hengel, *The Son of God.*

Hurtado, *Lord Jesus Christ.*

———, *One God, One Lord.*

Sanders, *Judaism Practice and Belief, 63 BCE–66 CE.*

Segal, *Two Powers in Heaven.*

Tobin, "Logos."

Vermes, *Jesus the Jew.*

Questions to Consider

1. Try to explain to your next-door neighbor, who knows nothing about religion, how a Jewish hypostasis works—both what it is and how it can be imagined to be God.

2. What strikes you as most peculiar about the fact that some humans in Judaism, such as the Jewish king, could be called "God"?

The Life and Teachings of Jesus
Lecture 6

The traditional Christian belief about Jesus, found among most Christians of most denominations throughout history, is that he is both fully God and fully man. Many Christians even today will say that this is what they believe, even though they do not think that Jesus really experienced the limitations involved with being a mortal human. In this lecture and the next, we will see that this understanding of Jesus as God does not go back to the lifetime of Jesus himself. Jesus did not call himself God or think of himself as God, and during his life, this is not what his followers thought of him either. The idea that Jesus was God came about only after Jesus's life and death.

Analyzing the Gospels
- We have already seen that scholars have wide-ranging understandings of who Jesus really was and what he really said, did, and experienced while living. Was he a great rabbi, a zealot rebel, a social reformer, a cynic philosopher, an apocalyptic prophet, or something else?

- The reason there have been so many disagreements about Jesus is that our earliest sources about his life—the New Testament Gospels—are not fully accurate representations of his words and deeds and are highly problematic for reconstructing the events of his life.
  o There are no other early sources for knowing about Jesus.

  o The Gospels are usually dated to 35 to 65 years after Jesus's death.

  o They were not written by eyewitnesses but by Greek-speaking Christians living outside of Palestine decades later.

- It is almost certain that the authors of the Gospels wrote down stories that had long been part of the oral tradition. As these stories had circulated by word of mouth over the decades since Jesus's death, they were changed—sometimes radically—and some were invented.

- This is why there are so many discrepancies in the Gospels, in their minor details, in their major claims, and in their overall portrayals of who Jesus was. As a result, scholars have had to establish rigorous historical criteria to help evaluate the Gospels as sources in order to determine what we can actually know about the life of the historical Jesus.

  o First, because stories of Jesus had been circulating for decades—and had been changed and invented—those that are found in a number of independent sources that have not been corroborated with one another are considered more likely to be historically accurate than those found in only one uncorroborated source.

  o Stories or sayings of Jesus that do not simply express what the Christian storytellers would have wanted to say about him or even that go against what later Christians said about him are more likely to be authentic—because those stories and sayings would not have been made up.

  o Any story or saying of Jesus must plausibly fit in the historical context within which he lived—1st-century Palestine—if it is to be accepted as historically accurate.

- Scholars who have applied these criteria do indeed come to different results, as we have seen. But one understanding of the historical Jesus has dominated scholarly discussions for more than a century now—and with good reason. That is the understanding that Jesus was, and understood himself to be, an apocalyptic prophet.

Apocalypticism

- Apocalypticism was an ancient Jewish theology that insisted that this world was controlled by forces of evil, but that God would soon intervene in history to overthrow those forces and usher in a good kingdom, in which there would be no more pain, misery, or suffering.
  - This view is called *apocalyptic* from the Greek word *apocalypsis*, which means a "revealing" or an "unveiling."

  - Jewish apocalypticists believed that God had revealed or unveiled to them the heavenly secrets of what was soon to take place on earth, when he would destroy all that were opposed to him and bring in his kingdom.

- This worldview was dominant in 1st-century Judaism, as we know from numerous Jewish writings of the time, including the Dead Sea Scrolls, a collection of documents, discovered in 1947, that were written by Jews living not too far from where Jesus lived and at about the same time.

- There are four major components to this ancient worldview, the first of which is dualism.
  - Apocalypticists believed that there were two forces in this world, good and evil, with everything and everyone (including supernatural powers) taking one side or the other.

  - This cosmic dualism had a historical component that was also dualistic: The present age is controlled by the forces of evil, but there is a good kingdom that is coming that will be controlled by God and his agents.

- The second component of apocalypticism was pessimism about the possibilities of life in this age, given that this age was controlled by evil powers.

- The third component was vindication. God was about to overthrow the evil powers and vindicate his name, his world, and his people.

- o God would intervene in history by sending a savior from heaven, sometimes called the Son of Man, who would destroy all that was opposed to God, judge all the people of earth, and punish God's enemies but reward his followers.

- o This judgment would come not only to those who were alive at the time but also to those who had already died. Apocalypticists developed and promoted the idea of the resurrection of the dead, when at the end of this age, all who had previously died would reenter their bodies to face judgment.

- Finally, the fourth component of apocalypticism was imminence—all this was to happen very soon. Apocalypticists believed that they were living at the very end of the age and that soon, this world would come to a crashing halt.

Jesus as Prophet

- Jesus of Nazareth himself appears to have held such views; these are the ideas that he proclaimed in our earliest surviving sources, especially our three earliest Gospels, Matthew, Mark, and Luke.

- Jesus's preaching focuses on the coming kingdom of God, a real kingdom on earth, where the righteous would be rewarded but

Like other Jews of his time, Jesus was an apocalypticist, believing that the kingdom of God was imminent.

the wicked excluded. This kingdom would be brought by the Son of Man, a cosmic judge from heaven.

- Jesus almost certainly did not think of himself as the Son of Man. It's true that in the Gospels, he calls himself by that name, but we must remember that the Gospels are Christian texts written by Christian authors. These authors had heard their stories about Jesus from Christian storytellers, and for decades, the stories, including the sayings of Jesus, had been changed.

- For reasons we will see in a later lecture, the later storytellers believed that Jesus was the Son of Man, and thus, naturally, when they told their stories about Jesus's teaching, he gives himself that name.

- But in some of Jesus's teachings, he appears to be talking about someone else. It is those sayings about the Son of Man that appear to go back to Jesus himself, not to his later followers.

- In these sayings, Jesus speaks about a future cosmic judge of the earth who would bring destruction, prior to the appearance of God's kingdom.
  - In the kingdom, there would be a reversal of fortunes: The last would be first and the first, last.

  - To enter the kingdom, people must obey God's will as expressed in Scripture, by loving their neighbors as themselves and by trusting God as a child trusts a good parent.

  - The twelve disciples would be rulers in the future kingdom.

  - The Son of Man was to appear very soon; the kingdom of God was imminent.

  - Those who followed Jesus's teachings of love and mercy and justice and compassion were already beginning to see what the kingdom would be like in the here and now.

- Jesus, in short, was a Jewish apocalypticist, one who expected the imminent end of history as we know it and the miraculous arrival of a judge from heaven, who would bring in God's utopian kingdom here on earth.

- But what did Jesus think about himself? Did he think that he was God on earth? We will address that question in the next lecture.

Suggested Reading

Allison, *Jesus of Nazareth*.

Collins, A., and J. J. Collins, *King and Messiah as Son of God*.

Collins, J. J. *The Apocalyptic Imagination*.

———, *The Star and Scepter*.

Ehrman, *How Jesus Became God: The Exaltation of a Jewish Preacher from Galilee*.

———, *Jesus: Apocalyptic Prophet of the New Millennium*.

Fredriksen, *From Jesus to Christ*.

———, *Jesus of Nazareth, King of the Jews*.

Meier, *A Marginal Jew*.

Sanders, *The Historical Figure of Jesus*.

Schweitzer, *The Quest of the Historical Jesus*.

Vermes, *Jesus the Jew*.

Questions to Consider

1. What are the leading characteristics of Jewish apocalyptic thinking?

2. How would you summarize the apocalyptic character of Jesus's own preaching?

Did Jesus Think He Was God?

Lecture 7

I n only one of the Gospels, the Gospel of John, the last of the four to be written, does Jesus declare himself to be God. In the earlier Synoptic Gospels, Matthew, Mark, and Luke, as we have seen, Jesus preaches about the coming kingdom of God, to be brought by a cosmic judge called the Son of Man. Even his ethical teachings in these Gospels must be situated in this apocalyptic context: Jesus's concern was that people should behave in ways that God desires so that they may enter the coming kingdom. Rarely did Jesus teach publicly about himself, and his public proclamations show that he considered himself a prophet of God, not God himself.

Jesus in the Gospel of John

- In the last of the New Testament Gospels to be written, the Gospel of John (c. 90–95 C.E.), Jesus makes a series of stunning declarations about himself, in which he indicates that he existed in eternity past in the glory of God and that he himself is equal with God.

- This is very different from anything Jesus says about himself in the earlier Gospels, Matthew, Mark, and Luke. These are called the Synoptic Gospels because they are so similar to one another that they can be "seen together"—the literal meaning of *synoptic*.
  - Mark is the earliest Gospel (c. 65–70 C.E.) and was used by Matthew and Luke for many of their stories about Jesus (c. 80–85 C.E.).

  - Matthew and Luke had other sources at their disposal, as well. Scholars have termed these sources as follows: Q, a hypothetical source used by both Matthew and Luke for their material not found in Mark; M, a source available to Matthew alone; and L, a source available to Luke alone.

- It is striking that Jesus never makes any claims to be divine in any of these earlier Gospels or their sources. How could that be if

John—our final Gospel—is correct that this was the very burden of his entire message? Did the earlier Gospels and their sources choose simply not to mention Jesus's divinity?

- Historians of the Gospels have long concluded that the idea that Jesus called himself God is not historical. If it were, it would be in the earliest Gospels; this is a view that is distinctive to John, the last of the Gospels to be written.

Jesus in the Synoptic Gospels

- As we have seen, in the Synoptic Gospels, Jesus preaches about the coming kingdom of God, to be brought by a cosmic judge that Jesus called the Son of Man. In these Gospels, Jesus rarely speaks about himself.

- He also speaks about how people should live, of course. Jesus is often seen as a great ethical teacher, one of the greatest moral instructors in the history of the world. But it's important to understand the apocalyptic character of Jesus's ethical teachings.

In the earliest and most reliable traditions about Jesus, he does not call himself God but instead presents himself as a human prophet.

  o Jesus did not teach ethics so that people would know how to get along over the long term. For him, there was not going to be a long term.

  o Instead, Jesus taught ethics so that people who lived as God wanted them to could enter the coming kingdom.

o Moreover, those who lived in these ways would begin to see what life would be like in that kingdom, where there would be no more war, hatred, oppression, injustice, poverty, or disease.

- In short, Jesus appears to have seen himself as a prophet of the coming kingdom, not as God on earth. Some people have argued that some of Jesus's actions show that he thought he was God, but in every case, these actions can be explained in other ways.
  o Is it true that Jesus performed miracles? Even if he did, this would not make him God any more than it would make any other miracle worker God—from the prophet Elijah of the Hebrew Bible, to Jesus's Jewish contemporary Hanina ben Dosa, to the modern-day Oral Roberts.

  o Is it true that Jesus forgave sins? Even if he did, this would not make him God any more than it would the Jewish priests who forgave sins in the name of God.

  o Is it true that people occasionally bowed down before Jesus in worship? Even if they did, this would not make him God any more than it would the thousands of kings in antiquity before whom people constantly bowed down.

The Messiah
- Jesus's preaching, rather than being about his own divinity, was about God's coming kingdom—and about God's coming king.

- In ancient Jewish tradition there was a term for the future king of Israel: *messiah*. The messiah was not supposed to be God but a human.

- The roots of the idea that there would be a future messiah go back to 2 Samuel 7:13–16, the promise of God to David that he would always have a descendant on the throne.

- This promise was nullified 500 years later, when the nation of Judah was destroyed and the Davidic king was removed from the throne, never to be reinstated.

- Later Jews thought that God would fulfill his promise to David and, in the future, once more place a descendant of David on the throne. This would be a human king, just as David had been a human king.

- The kings of Israel were sometimes called "God's anointed one." In the Hebrew language, the word for "anointed one" is *mashiach*, from which we get *messiah*. The Greek form of that word is *christos*, from which we get the word *Christ*.

- For most Jews, the coming messiah/Christ was not to be a divine figure but a human figure. Note that no Jew ever thought the messiah was God.
  - Moreover, we have no record of any Jew thinking that the messiah was someone who would die for the sake of others and then be raised from the dead. That is what later Christians said the messiah was supposed to do, based on their views that Jesus was the messiah and that he had died and been raised.

  - But prior to Christianity, no Jew thought this. In no passage of the Hebrew Bible that mentions the messiah is there any reference to a death and resurrection, and among no Jewish interpreters of the Bible was there any sense that this was to be the fate of the messiah. The messiah was to be a great and powerful figure who overthrew the enemy and established God's kingdom on earth.

- Jesus, too, expected a future figure to be the messiah, a human ruler of God's kingdom, and saw himself not as God but as the prophet at the end of time, predicting that the messiah was soon to appear.

Suggested Reading

Allison, *Jesus of Nazareth*.

Ehrman, *How Jesus Became God: The Exaltation of a Jewish Preacher from Galilee*.

———, *Jesus: Apocalyptic Prophet of the New Millennium*.

Fredriksen, *From Jesus to Christ*.

———, *Jesus of Nazareth, King of the Jews*.

Meier, *A Marginal Jew*.

Sanders, *The Historical Figure of Jesus*.

Schweitzer, *The Quest of the Historical Jesus*.

Vermes, *Jesus the Jew*.

Questions to Consider

1. Why do you suppose our latest Gospel, John, indicates that Jesus declared himself equal with God when we don't find such sayings in our earliest Gospels of Matthew, Mark, and Luke?

2. What was the Jewish messiah supposed to be like?

The Death of Jesus—Historical Certainties
Lecture 8

The most well-documented period of Jesus's life are the days before his Crucifixion, and a major key to understanding him is to know about the events that led up to his death. In this lecture, we will discuss what we know with relative certainty about these events; in the next lecture, we'll discuss a matter of equal importance, namely, what we simply cannot know. At the outset, we can say that there are two virtually certain facts about Jesus's death, which occurred in or around the year 30 C.E.: (1) He was crucified by the Romans on the orders of the Roman governor of Judea, Pontius Pilate, and (2) The charges against him were political—that he had been calling himself king of the Jews.

Jesus at the Feast of Passover
- In considering the events leading up to Jesus's Crucifixion, it is important to remember that the historian can never simply take what is said in one of the Gospels—especially the Gospel of John— at face value as giving historically reliable information. We need to look especially at our earliest sources—the Synoptics—and apply the historical criteria to them that we discussed in Lecture 6. When we do so, we can learn a good deal about Jesus's last days.

- It is virtually certain that Jesus spent almost his entire public ministry in the northern part of the land, in Galilee, proclaiming the coming kingdom of God. It is also virtually certain that in the last week of his life, he made a trip to Jerusalem with his disciples to celebrate the feast of Passover.
  - Passover was—and is—an annual festival celebrated by Jews to commemorate the formative event of the nation of Israel: its escape from slavery in Egypt under the powerful hand of Moses.

  - The event involved a special meal consisting of symbolic foods that helped the participants remember the story, as told in the book of Exodus in the Hebrew Bible. Many Jews believed that to celebrate it properly required them to come to Jerusalem and participate in the sacrifice of the Passover lambs in the Temple, lambs that were then taken home and eaten at the Passover meal.

- The size of Jerusalem swelled many times over during the Passover festival, and it was a time of tension and danger, especially for the Roman occupiers of the land of Israel.
  o The festival commemorated the time when God had saved Israel from the oppressive hand of a foreign power, and many Jews participated in the feast not merely looking back to what God had done under Moses but also to what he would do to deliver them from Rome.

  o The Romans understood this full well. This was the one time of year when the Roman governor would come to the city from his residence in Caesarea, bringing troops to station around the city to quell any possible riots.

- In all of our sources, in the last week of Jesus's life, he went to Jerusalem to celebrate Passover. But why did he go?
  o Was it to die for the sins of the world? That would be a theological answer.

  o A historical answer is not difficult to find. Jesus had been proclaiming his message in the remote, rural areas of Galilee; he was now bringing his message to the heart of the Jewish nation, the Jewish people, and the Jewish religion—to Jerusalem at Passover.

  o Evidence that this was his purpose is found in the Gospels: It is during this week that he preaches most forcefully his message of the coming destruction to be brought by the Son of Man before the appearance of God's future kingdom.

Events in Jerusalem

- There is also little doubt about what Jesus did when he first arrived in the city of Jerusalem, on what was possibly his first visit. He entered the enormous Temple compound, found what was happening there disturbing, and began to overturn the tables and attack some of the Jews who were helping to run the Temple cult.

- Was Jesus upset that some Jews were using the Temple cult to make money off of religion?

- Some scholars have maintained that Jesus's actions in the Temple were a kind of enacted parable, showing what would happen when the Son of Man arrived: All those who were against God—including the leadership of the Jews in Jerusalem—would be destroyed.

- It is no wonder that these Jewish leaders—who probably had never heard of Jesus before—did not take kindly to him or his message. And they no doubt saw that his actions could indeed create a following; the masses were eager to hear how God was soon to intervene in their situation.

- Thus, the Jewish leaders—the chief priests and the members of the ruling council (the Sanhedrin)—kept a close eye on Jesus. Ultimately, they believed they had to act to remove him from the public eye. But how were they to do so without causing a disturbance that could lead to even more trouble?

Jesus's Betrayal

- Our sources are consistent in stating that the Jewish authorities bribed one of Jesus's closest disciples, Judas Iscariot, to betray him. This view passes our various historical criteria, but a question remains: Did Judas simply tell the authorities Jesus's whereabouts when the crowds were not present? It seems that there may have been more involved in Judas's betrayal.

- We must take into account several striking pieces of information.

© jozef sedmak/iStock/Thinkstock.

It seems likely that Judas told the Roman authorities more than just Jesus's whereabouts; he may have betrayed teachings that Jesus had given to his disciples in private.

o   First, there is no doubt that Jesus was killed by the Romans, not the Jews, and that his execution was for political treason—for calling himself the king of the Jews.

o   Jesus was not the only Jew from antiquity who claimed to be the messiah; the Romans reacted violently against all such messianic claimants, routinely killing them for political insurgency.

o   But what is striking is that Jesus is never recorded as calling himself king of the Jews in any of his public proclamations.

Why would he be crucified for something he never called himself?

- We are repeatedly told in the Gospels that Jesus taught his own disciples privately. And we have a good indication of one thing he taught them: a saying that appears in Matthew and Luke (meaning that it comes from the early source Q) that no later Christian would have made up; thus, this teaching is almost certainly historical. Jesus told his disciples that they would be the rulers of the Twelve Tribes of Israel in the future kingdom.
  - But if the disciples were rulers, who would rule them? The answer was that Jesus was their leader now. He was the one who had called them. It was by following his teaching that they would enter the kingdom.

  - It appears that Jesus taught the disciples that just as he ruled them now, so, too, would he rule them later—that when the Son of Man arrived, Jesus himself would be made king of the coming kingdom. And this would happen within their own lifetimes, when he was made messiah of the coming kingdom.

  - This is the secret that Judas betrayed. Judas told the authorities that Jesus was calling himself the future king of the Jews.

- For this reason, when the authorities became fearful of a riot, they had Jesus taken into custody and handed him over to Pontius Pilate for trial.
  - Pilate would not have cared if Jesus disagreed with the Jewish authorities on matters of the Jewish religion or if he had ever committed religious blasphemy. Pilate was a Roman governor of a Roman province, and he cared only for threats to Rome.

  - The charge against Jesus was that he was claiming to usurp the power of Rome, claiming to be the future king when only the Romans could appoint the king.

o   Pilate evidently questioned Jesus about whether he called himself the king of the Jews, and Jesus either did not respond or answered truthfully, that he was to be the future king.

o   That is all Pilate had to know. He ordered Jesus to be crucified. Jesus was flogged and taken to the cross, and according to our earliest records, he was dead within six hours.

The Aftermath

- The death of Jesus must have radically disconfirmed for the disciples what they had thought of him.

- It is important to realize that no ancient Jew imagined that the messiah would be one who would die for the sake of others. Instead, the messiah was to be the great and powerful deliverer of his people from their foreign oppressor.

- During Jesus's lifetime, his disciples may have thought that he was to be king of the coming kingdom—the great and powerful messiah—but after his death, it seemed clear that he was not. He had not overthrown the enemy but was destroyed by the enemy. He had not established a new kingdom but was executed by the rulers of the present kingdom.

- The death of Jesus must have sent his followers into despair, a despair that would only disappear—in a glorious way—when they came to think that God had raised him from the dead.

Suggested Reading

Allison, *Jesus of Nazareth*.

Brown, *The Death of the Messiah*.

Collins, A., and J. J. Collins, *King and Messiah as Son of God*.

Collins, J. J. *The Star and Scepter*.

Ehrman, *How Jesus Became God: The Exaltation of a Jewish Preacher from Galilee.*

———, *Jesus: Apocalyptic Prophet of the New Millennium.*

Fredriksen, *From Jesus to Christ.*

———, *Jesus of Nazareth, King of the Jews.*

Meier, *A Marginal Jew.*

Sanders, *The Historical Figure of Jesus.*

Schweitzer, *The Quest of the Historical Jesus.*

Vermes, *Jesus the Jew.*

Questions to Consider

1. Why was the Passover a particularly incendiary and dangerous time for a popular preacher to make his appearance in Jerusalem?

2. What were the charges made against Jesus at his trial, and what was the basis for them (that is, why was he charged with such things)?

Jesus's Death—What Historians Can't Know
Lecture 9

In the previous lecture, we discussed what historians can know with reasonable certainty about Jesus's death; in this lecture, we look at the flip side of that coin, what we cannot know about his death. This discussion will serve as a prelude to the following two lectures, which deal with what we can and cannot know about his Resurrection. Those lectures are the keys to the entire course; in them, we will see that it was precisely the belief that God had raised Jesus from the dead that led his followers to claim that he was, in fact, God.

Discrepancies in the Sources
- There are some events leading up to Jesus's death that we cannot know about because the sources are so full of discrepancies, both major and minor. This is no real surprise, given that these sources are all based on oral traditions that had been in circulation for decades.

- Some of these discrepancies are important and difficult to reconcile. For example, what day was Jesus crucified?
  o Mark is quite unambiguous. Jesus was crucified on the day after the Passover meal was eaten.

  o John is also quite unambiguous. Jesus was crucified on the day before the Passover meal was eaten.

  o Why does the day matter? Because John has clearly changed a historical fact in order to make a theological point. For him (and only him), Jesus was the "lamb of God who takes away the sins of the world" (John 1:29). Thus, it is not an accident that in John's account, Jesus is killed on the same day, by the same people, who killed the Passover lambs.

- o This is the problem of the historical reliability of the Gospels in a nutshell: These writers, and the storytellers who preceded them, are less interested in giving historically accurate facts than in giving theologically interpreted stories. This is why historians must use these accounts so carefully, applying rigorous historical criteria.

- There are other issues in the Gospel stories of the events leading up to Jesus's death that are familiar but highly problematic from a historical standpoint. A good example is his supposed triumphal entry into Jerusalem to the acclaims of the masses that he was the one coming "in the name of the Lord."
  - o This is, in effect, the acclamation that Jesus is the coming messiah.

  - o If in fact any such thing had happened, it is difficult to explain why Jesus would not have been arrested on the spot by the Roman troops. After all, they had been brought into town precisely to prevent any such enthusiastic acclamation that could lead to civil disturbances.

Jesus's Burial
- Perhaps the most significant historical problem in the accounts of Jesus's death is the question of whether or not he was given a decent burial.

- In all four Gospels, Jesus is said to have been buried by a Jewish leader named Joseph of Arimathea, a member of the Sanhedrin.

- There are indeed other reports of how Jesus was buried, including Acts 13:28–29, which may preserve an older tradition. As the tradition developed, storytellers provided "names for the nameless."

- It's important to reflect on why storytellers would want to make sure it was understood that Jesus was given a decent burial in a known tomb.

© TonyBaggett/iStock/Thinkstock.

Early Christian storytellers would have wanted to claim that Jesus was buried in a specific tomb to support the claim that he had been raised from the dead.

- o If Jesus did not have a known tomb, then no one could later claim that the tomb was empty, and the claim of an empty tomb eventually became a central aspect of the Christian proclamation that Jesus had been raised from the dead. One piece of proof was that he was no longer in his tomb.

- o But what if he was never placed in a tomb?

- There are three reasons for thinking that Jesus was never given a decent burial in a tomb that could be identified.
  - o It was against Roman practices to allow crucified criminals to be given decent burials. Instead, they were left to rot for days on their crosses as part of the punishment.

- o Romans usually buried lowly criminals themselves—rather than allowing others to do so—in common graves. With this burial method, if the corpses were not already disintegrated beyond recognition and identification, they would be in a matter of days.

- o Pontius Pilate in particular was not a sympathetic ruler who was willing to bestow kindnesses on those who asked.

What We Can and Cannot Know
- In the end, as historians, we must realize that there are numerous incidents in the Gospels that we cannot know about or that we cannot accept as historically certain.

- What is certain is that Jesus was executed by Pilate for calling himself the king of the Jews. This unexpected turn of events must have driven the disciples of Jesus into deep despair until they came to believe that God had reversed the judgment of the world by raising Jesus from the dead. This reversal led the disciples to begin to proclaim that far from being a discredited messiah, Jesus had been made divine.

Suggested Reading

Allison, *Jesus of Nazareth*.

Brown, *The Death of the Messiah*.

Ehrman, *How Jesus Became God: The Exaltation of a Jewish Preacher from Galilee*.

———, *Jesus: Apocalyptic Prophet of the New Millennium*.

Fredriksen, *From Jesus to Christ*.

———, *Jesus of Nazareth, King of the Jews*.

Meier, *A Marginal Jew*.

Sanders, *The Historical Figure of Jesus*.

Schweitzer, *The Quest of the Historical Jesus*.

Vermes, *Jesus the Jew*.

Questions to Consider

1. Why is it that historians cannot trust that all of the stories of Jesus's last days, as recounted in the New Testament Gospels, are historically accurate?

2. What are the arguments for and against Jesus's body having been given a decent burial in a known tomb after his Crucifixion?

The Resurrection—What Historians Can't Know

Lecture 10

W ithout a doubt, the Resurrection of Jesus stands as the lynchpin for the entire Christian faith. If no one had ever come to believe that Jesus had been raised from the dead, Christianity would probably never have existed. Given the fundamental importance of the Resurrection for the beginning of Christianity and for understanding Jesus himself as a divine figure, it is necessary for us to ask: What can we know about the Resurrection historically? What can historians say about what happened to make the disciples come to believe that Jesus was raised from the dead? And what can historians not say about this key event that ended up changing the history of the world?

Centrality of the Resurrection
- The Resurrection of Jesus is obviously central to the Christian faith. Indeed, if no one had ever come to believe that Jesus had been raised from the dead, there probably never would have been any such thing as Christianity.

- During his lifetime, Jesus himself was a Jew, and his followers were Jews. Jesus preached a Jewish message based on his understanding of the Jewish Scripture and the Jewish God. He proclaimed that in his own generation, God would intervene in history to destroy the forces of evil and establish his long-awaited kingdom on earth.

- If Jesus had been arrested and crucified for crimes against the state and no one ever came to think that God had raised him from the dead, he would have been, at best, a footnote in Jewish history, another ill-advised prophet who made predictions that never came true and paid the price for it with his life. His followers would merely have been a small sect within Judaism that would have died out in time.

- It was the belief in the Resurrection that changed everything. Once the disciples of Jesus came to think that God had raised him from the dead, they understood everything he had ever said and done in a new light.

- Recall that in the ancient world, someone who was exalted to heaven and sat on a throne next to God was himself seen as divine. And that's what the disciples immediately came to see Jesus as—a divine being.
  o Jesus had taught that the Son of Man was soon to come from heaven to earth; after his death, his disciples said that Jesus was that Son of Man.

  o Jesus had taught that he would be the king of the future kingdom, the messiah; his disciples now said that he was already the king, not just of Israel but of the whole world, the Lord of heaven and earth.

  o Jesus had presented himself as a prophet who knew God's will; his disciples began to say that he was far more than that— that he had been exalted up to heaven by God and that he was sitting on God's throne as a divine being himself.

  o This was the beginning of the proclamation that Jesus was God.

History versus the Past
- Given the fundamental importance of the Resurrection, what can we say about it as historians? To answer this question, we need to look at the historical method and at what historians can and cannot demonstrate about the past.

- The first point to note may seem a bit confusing, but it is of central importance: History is not the past.
  o When we talk about "the past," we mean everything that has ever happened before now. When we talk about "history," we mean everything that we can show has happened before now.

These are obviously not the same thing because most of the past cannot be shown to have happened with anything like proof.

o   In some cases, we lack adequate sources. For example, we cannot show historically what my grandfather ate for lunch on March 3, 1951. That event is in the past; it almost certainly happened, but we have no access to it.

o   There are other things we cannot show historically simply because they are not the kinds of things that history can show. For example, history cannot show that the square root of 144 is 12. That is a mathematical question, and if you know that it's true, it's not because you've done a historical investigation, but because you've done the math. Further, history does not have access to internal emotional states.

o   Thus, the past is everything that happened (what my grandfather ate at one time, the fact that you answered a mathematical question correctly, and so on), and history is what can be shown to have happened in the past.

Historians' Presuppositions

•   Among the things that history cannot show happened in the past are miracles, including the miracle of the Resurrection. This is not because historians must be secular humanists with anti-supernaturalist biases, as some Christian apologists sometimes claim.

•   Instead, there are two reasons that historians cannot demonstrate that miracles happened—even if they did happen. The first has to do with the presuppositions that historians bring to their work when they are working as historians.

o   All of us have presuppositions. The question is: What kinds of presupposition are appropriate for the task at hand? When it comes to reconstructing the past—which is the work of the historian—some presuppositions are acceptable and others are not.

- o Historians presuppose, for example, that the past did happen. There's no way to prove that it did, but historians assume, just like virtually everyone else, that it really did happen.

- o Historians also presuppose that there are ways of showing what is likely to have happened in the past—primarily by appealing to historical sources and criteria.

- Other presuppositions are not appropriate for historians for the simple reason that they are not shared by other historians engaged in the investigation.
  - o For example, historians—when they are engaged in doing history—cannot conclude that the Mormon religion started when the angel Moroni appeared to Joseph Smith and revealed to him the golden tablets. That event may have occurred, but believing that it did requires the historian to believe that angels exist, that Joseph Smith had a revelation from an angel, and so on. Those are theological beliefs that are not shared by everyone, and thus, they cannot be among the presuppositions of the historian.

  - o The same thing applies to belief in the Resurrection. Even if it is a past event, it cannot be established historically because it presupposes matters of belief that are not shared by all investigators.

Historical Probability
- The other problem with trying to prove on historical grounds that a miracle happened is that one of the presuppositions appropriate to historical inquiry is that it can establish only what probably happened in the past.

- We cannot prove the past in the same way we can prove a scientific experiment. Thus, historians establish levels of probability for the past based on surviving evidence. Some events are so highly probable that we may call them certain; others are very probable, fairly probable, possible, unlikely, and so on.

- The problem with miracles is that they are, by definition, if not impossible, then possible only in the most infinitesimally remote degree. Otherwise, they wouldn't be miraculous. Many people believe that Jesus walked on water, but they would also admit that such an event happens so rarely that it must be called miraculous.

- Historians, though, can establish only what probably happened in the past, and if miracles are by definition the least probable occurrence, then historians cannot show they happened.

- This does not mean that historians must be nonbelievers. It means if they believe in miracles, it is on the basis of faith, not on the basis of historical knowledge.

- In short, even if Jesus was raised from the dead in the past, there is no way for historians to show it historically. People who think that he was raised think so not because of historical evidence, but because that is their belief.

The Tradition of the Resurrection

- Even though we cannot establish historically that God raised Jesus from the dead, there are some things we can say about the traditions of Jesus's Resurrection from a historical standpoint. Some of these things are historically unlikely, and others are probable. One thing that is virtually certain, as we will see in the next lecture, is that whether or not Jesus was actually raised from the dead, some of his followers believed he was.

- Other things, however, are not so certain. For example, we have already seen that it is unlikely that Jesus was buried in a known tomb. Thus, it is also unlikely that the tomb was discovered by his followers to be empty.

- We also don't know when the disciples first said that Jesus was raised from the dead. The tradition in the Gospels indicates that it was three days later, but that's difficult to know.

There are a number of traditions surrounding Christ's Resurrection that historians cannot establish, including the discovery of the empty tomb and the identity of the first people to believe he had been resurrected.

- o If the Gospels are correct that the disciples fled from Jesus at the time of his arrest, it's likely that they would have returned to Galilee, a seven-day walk from Jerusalem.

- o If they came to believe that Jesus was raised once they were in Galilee—as suggested by Mark (and indicated by Matthew)— then this belief emerged at least a week later and possibly much more than that.

- It is also impossible to know who was the first to believe that Jesus had been raised from the dead. Different sources suggest different people: Paul indicates it was Peter; the Gospels suggest it was Mary Magdalene.

- Finally, it is impossible to know how many of the disciples of Jesus came to believe that he had been raised. According to the Gospels, it was all of the remaining disciples, along with Jesus's female followers from Galilee. But it is striking that in every instance in which Jesus appears to his disciples in the Gospels, some or all of them doubt. This may be most easily explained on the grounds that some of Jesus's followers never did come to believe in the Resurrection.

- In short, historians cannot establish that God raised Jesus from the dead, although theologians, with their different sets of presuppositions, may well argue that he was, and believers certainly think he was. But this is not a historical claim—even if it did happen in the past. It is a theological or religious claim. In addition, there are many aspects of the stories of Jesus's Resurrection that are highly doubtful, but there are also some things that are certain, and those are what we will discuss in the next lecture.

Suggested Reading

Allison, *Resurrecting Jesus*.

Brown, *The Virginal Conception and Bodily Resurrection of Jesus*.

Ehrman, *How Jesus Became God: The Exaltation of a Jewish Preacher from Galilee*.

———, *Jesus: Apocalyptic Prophet of the New Millennium*.

Fredriksen, *From Jesus to Christ*.

———, *Jesus of Nazareth, King of the Jews*.

Goulder, "The Baseless Fabric of a Vision."

Lüdemann, *The Resurrection of Christ*.

1. Discuss the presuppositions that strike you as appropriate and those that strike you as inappropriate for historians trying to establish what happened in the past.

2. Do you agree that historians—acting as historians, with appropriate historical assumptions—cannot establish whether a miracle, such as Jesus's Resurrection, actually happened or not? Why or why not?

What History Reveals about the Resurrection
Lecture 11

Even though we, as historians, cannot provide historical proof for a miracle, such as the Resurrection of Jesus, there are certain things we can say about this pivotal event that marks the beginning of Christianity. Above all, we can say that whether or not Jesus was actually raised from the dead, some of his disciples claimed that he was. What made some of Jesus's followers believe that he had been resurrected? The simple answer is one that is attested in all of our earliest sources: Some followers of Jesus had visions of him alive after his death. This is a historical explanation that can be accepted by believers and unbelievers alike on purely historical grounds.

The Start of Christianity

- Contrary to what we might think, the Christian religion did not begin with the life and teaching of Jesus. Christianity started out as a belief in Jesus's Resurrection; if the followers of Jesus had simply adhered to his teaching, they would have remained as one of the sects of Judaism.

- We cannot say either that Christianity started with Jesus's death because without the Resurrection, his death would simply have been seen as the death of yet another Jewish prophet who ended up on the wrong side of the law.

- Nor, technically speaking, can we say that Christianity started with Jesus's Resurrection—both because historians cannot demonstrate, on historical grounds, that Jesus was raised from the dead and because if Jesus had been raised but no one knew about it, then there would have been no faith in his Resurrection.

- Thus, Christianity started with the proclamation of Jesus's Resurrection by some of his followers. What is it that made these followers believe that Jesus had been raised from the dead?

Belief in the Resurrection

- It's important to stress that belief in Jesus's Resurrection was not based on the fact that there was an empty tomb. As we've seen, it is doubtful, from a historical standpoint, that there was an empty tomb. Further, an empty tomb would not make someone think that Jesus had been raised from the dead because there are other, more obvious explanations for why a tomb would be empty.

- Even more significant, all of our earliest sources are unified in saying that it was visions of Jesus alive—not the empty tomb—that made his followers believe he had been raised.
  - Our earliest account is in the writings of Paul: 1 Corinthians 15:3–8. It is widely recognized that this account is a *pre-literary formula*, that is, a saying that existed prior to its being incorporated into its current literary context. It is a view of the faith that predates Paul's founding of the church in Corinth, as Paul himself indicates.

  - As such, Paul's account may be the earliest record we have of why it is that people came to believe in the Resurrection—an account written decades before the Gospels.

  - And this passage is completely unambiguous: It was the so-called "appearances" of Jesus to his followers that led them to believe. There is no reference here to an empty tomb.

  - The same is true of the Gospels. In the Gospel of Luke (24:3, 11; 13–53), the discovery of the empty tomb does not inspire anyone to believe that Jesus was raised; it is only when he appears to them that they come to believe. We can make a similar point about the Gospel of John (20:1–13; 14–18).

- Our earliest sources, then, are quite definite: It was visions of Jesus alive again, after his death, that inspired the belief that he had been raised from the dead.

- How can we accept that as a historical explanation? Doesn't the claim that his disciples saw Jesus alive after he had died require the historian to accept the miracle of the Resurrection—something that cannot be accepted on historical grounds?
  - The answer is no. On the contrary, it is perfectly possible for historians to accept the premise that Jesus's followers declared that Jesus had been brought back to life based on visions of him they had because people have visions all the time.

  - Sometimes people have visions that scholars would call *veridical*—meaning they actually saw what they thought they saw—and other times, visions are *nonveridical*—meaning that the person experiencing the vision had a hallucination.

  - In other words, sometimes we see someone in our bedroom at night because someone is really there, and at other times, we're just seeing things.

- Believers in Jesus's physical Resurrection would say that the disciples' visions of Jesus were veridical; nonbelievers would say that they were nonveridical. But in either case, the historian can say that it was the visions that made the followers of Jesus believe he was still alive.

- New Testament scholars themselves are split on the question of whether the visions were veridical or not. Some, such as Mike Licona and N. T. Wright, insist that Jesus really did appear to his disciples after his death, and others, such as Michael Goulder and Gerd Lüdemann, insist that the disciples had hallucinations.

- As historians, we do not need to resolve that matter. We will look at the phenomenon of nonveridical visions further in our next lecture. For now, we will explore what more we can say about belief in the Resurrection of Jesus based on visionary experiences.

© Steven Wynn/iStock/Thinkstock.

The Gospel of John includes the story of doubting Thomas, who required physical proof of the Resurrection.

Visions of Jesus

- It is impossible to know how many of Jesus's disciples actually had visions of him after his death. The Gospels, of course, indicate that all of the 11 remaining disciples, as well as several of Jesus's female followers, had these visions, and as a result, all of them believed. There are reasons, however, to call these accounts into question.

- Most striking, there are consistent reports in the Gospels that some of the disciples "doubted" that Jesus actually appeared to them, calling for proof from the resurrected Jesus (thus, Matthew 28:17; Luke 24:10–11; John 20; and Acts 1:3).

- Why would the disciples experience doubt if, in fact, Jesus was right in front of them talking to them? This is a particularly pressing question because, as we will see in the next lecture, people who have visions of deceased loved ones almost never doubt what they have seen.

- One explanation for the doubting tradition is that these stories of doubt were told to explain why some of the disciples never came to believe.
    - A plausible situation is this: Some of the disciples—but not all of them—had these visions. Peter is universally said to have had one, as is Mary Magdalene. And we know that later, the apostle Paul did, as well.

    - These three people—Peter, Paul, and Mary—told of their visions to others. Many believed them, but others were not so sure, as is seen in the later stories of the doubting disciples.

    - This would also explain why we have passages that indicate Jesus is sometimes not "recognized" by those having the vision.

Understandings of the Resurrection
- If some of the disciples had visions of Jesus alive after his death, and therefore, they came to believe that he was no longer dead, how would they understand his Resurrection? In fact, different early Christians had different understandings of what it meant to say that Jesus was raised.

- Some Christians, including some of Paul's opponents in some of his churches, claimed that Jesus's body, in fact, had not been raised at all. Instead, he had been raised in spirit, while his body experienced corruption, like all other bodies.

- Paul insisted, on the contrary, that Jesus's body had experienced a spiritual resurrection: The body itself was raised, but it was raised as an "immortal" body—glorified, no longer subject to the limitations, failings, and temporalities of human bodies.

- Other Christians insisted even more vehemently than Paul on the real physical nature of the Resurrection—that the body that came out of the grave was precisely the body that went into it, as seen in the stories of the Resurrection in the later Gospels of Luke and John.

- What would the earliest followers of Jesus—his own disciples—have thought?

   o   It is important to remember that the disciples were, like Jesus, apocalypticists. They, like him, thought that at the end of the age, everyone would be raised from the dead, bodily, to face judgment. Those who had done evil would be punished eternally, and those who had sided with God would be rewarded with eternal bliss.

   o   What would Jewish apocalypticists think if they believed that someone had been raised from the dead? One answer is that they would think the end was very near indeed—the resurrection had started! This would intensify the fervor of their belief, as they enthusiastically proclaimed that the kingdom was soon to appear on earth.

   o   In addition, for the disciples, the realization that Jesus had been raised certainly would have meant that his body had been reanimated and made glorious—as was to happen to all bodies at the end of the age and as Paul himself appears to have believed soon afterward.

   o   Thus, the earliest Christians, including Jesus's own followers, probably believed that Jesus's body had been raised and made eternal. He himself, in the body, had been made divine.

Suggested Reading

Allison, *Resurrecting Jesus*.

Brown, *An Introduction to the New Testament*.

———, *The Virginal Conception and Bodily Resurrection of Jesus*.

Ehrman, *How Jesus Became God: The Exaltation of a Jewish Preacher from Galilee.*

———, *Jesus: Apocalyptic Prophet of the New Millennium.*

Fredriksen, *From Jesus to Christ.*

———, *Jesus of Nazareth, King of the Jews.*

Goulder, "The Baseless Fabric of a Vision."

Lüdemann, *The Resurrection of Christ.*

Questions to Consider

1. Do you agree that the discovery of Jesus's empty tomb had no bearing on whether his followers came to think he was raised from the dead? Why or why not?

2. What is the evidence that visions of Jesus after his death led his followers to think he had been raised?

The Disciples' Visions of Jesus
Lecture 12

In the last lecture, we saw that even though historians cannot prove, on historical grounds, that Jesus was raised from the dead, it is relatively certain that his followers claimed that he had been, based on visionary experiences some of them had. These claims, as we will see, are not only the basis for the beginning of the Christian religion, but they are also the basis for a new understanding of Christ. From this point on, he was understood not as a mere mortal but as, in some sense, God.

Scientific Studies of Visions

- Can historians really say anything about visionary experiences? In fact, they can because we have documented and scientifically examined accounts of visions from the past.

- The first major study of visionary experiences was conducted near the end of the 19th century by a scholar named H. A. Sidgwick. He interviewed more than 15,000 men and women and determined that 7.8 percent of the men and 12 percent of the women had had at least one vivid hallucinatory experience (that is, a vision that Sidgwick judged to be nonveridical).

- The most comprehensive modern survey was undertaken by A. Y. Tien in 1991. In his analysis of more than 18,000 people, some 13 percent claimed to have had at least one vivid hallucination.

- How does one explain these large numbers—the fact that one out of every eight people seem to have had some kind of visionary experience taken to be real?

- Psychologist Richard Bentall explains that it is related to a skill all of us have called *source monitoring*.
  - This is a skill that we all use all the time to differentiate between self-generated events—that is, sensations that occur within our

own heads—and externally generated ones—sensations caused by external stimuli.

o   Bentall argues that like all skills, source monitoring fails on occasion; at those times, what is happening only in our heads is vividly but mistakenly taken to refer to something that occurs externally.

o   This source-monitoring skill is very much tied to the environment in which we live: If we have been raised in a society that subscribes to the existence of ghosts or the reality of dead people reappearing among us, then the chance that what one "sees" will be assumed to be a ghost or a dead person is heightened.

o   Moreover—and this is a key point—stress and emotional arousal can have a serious effect on source-monitoring skills, making us more susceptible to a breakdown in our ability to differentiate between internal and external processes. This is especially true in times of deep grief, trauma, or personal anguish.

o   Bentall, of course, is not referring to visions in the distant past, but for those of us interested in the visions of Jesus's followers, Bentall's findings are significant because, if nothing else, the disciples of Jesus, after his death, were experiencing deep grief, trauma, and personal anguish.

o   It is striking, in this connection, that the two most frequently reported visions that people have are of significant religious figures and loved ones who have been lost. We can examine both kinds of visions, based on modern research.

Visions of the Virgin

- One common vision in the modern age of a significant religious figure involves the mother of Jesus, the Virgin Mary, who regularly appears to people, sometimes to multiple people at one time, in extremely well-documented cases.

- A number of visions have been discussed by René Laurentin, a Catholic theologian who has a degree in philosophy from the Sorbonne in Paris and two doctorates, one in theology and one in literature. He has written many books describing the visions of Mary in the modern world.

- One example involves a set of appearances in 1984, in which a large group of people—more than 1,000 at one time—saw Mary appear near a local waterfall; these included doctors, lawyers, psychologists, and psychiatrists, nearly 500 of whom were personally interviewed and described their experience. Obviously, religious visions are not experienced only by uneducated and illiterate peasants.

The shrine to the Virgin Mary in Lourdes, France, marks the spot where a young girl was said to have had numerous visions of Mary.

- A large number of Marian apparitions are documented in such places as Lourdes, France; Garabandal, Spain; and Fátima, Portugal.
  - o In Fátima, for example, more than 50,000 people attested to the "cosmic miracle of the sun" on October 13, 1917, during which the sun began to spin wildly and tumble down to earth, radiating indescribably beautiful colors. This miracle was attributed to Mary.

  - o One sometimes hears that Jesus must actually have appeared to the disciples because Paul indicates that 500 brethren saw him at one time, and mass hallucinations are impossible. But if such hallucinations are impossible, then the sun actually must have fallen toward the earth in 1917; this miracle was seen not by 500 people but by 50,000.

Bereavement Visions
- Another type of exceedingly common vision is the bereavement vision, in which a deceased person appears to a loved one, convincing the visionary that the deceased is still, in some sense, alive.
  - These types of visions occur most frequently—but not always—with departed family members. The deceased person appears, speaks to, or touches the living person—or does all three.

  - In almost every recorded instance, the person who has had the vision is convinced that his or her loved one is still alive and is well, even knowing, of course, that the body has died.

  - These kinds of visions happen most commonly when the deceased was especially beloved; when his or her death was sudden, unexpected, or violent; and when the visionary feels guilt over how the loved one had been treated.

- An interesting and large set of anecdotal evidence has been collected by Bill and Judy Guggenheim in an account of what they call *after-death communications*.
  - The Guggenheims are not trained psychologists, and the anecdotes they have collected cannot be used for a scientific analysis for scholarly purposes.

  - But they are extremely important for seeing what people actually say about such experiences. The Guggenheims collected more than 3,500 accounts from people who claimed they were contacted by dead loved ones.

  - Even when the contact came in a dream, invariably, the visionaries accepted it as real, not as an event of their psyches.

o   In fact, the most striking feature of virtually all the stories is that the person who had the experience almost never doubted that the deceased had, in fact, initiated the contact and that the vision showed beyond all doubt that the person lived on and was doing well.

o   These visions could take place soon after the loved one had died, but sometimes they took place two or even three years later.

o   Again, these visions occur most frequently when the visionary is physically and emotionally exhausted, and they are more common when the person has died unexpectedly or tragically. Strikingly, many people don't think such things happen or even know about them happening until they have the experience.

•   The similarities between these common modern-day experiences and the visions of Jesus experienced by his followers cannot be missed.

o   In Jesus's case, we note the violent and sudden death of a deeply loved teacher—one for whom the disciples had given up everything in order to follow.

o   Jesus was suddenly and brutally taken away from the disciples, publicly humiliated, tortured, and crucified.

o   And the disciples had plenty of reasons for feeling guilt and shame over how they had failed Jesus both during his life and at his greatest time of need, at the very end.

•   Soon after his death, some of Jesus's followers had visions of him, as people do. They were deeply comforted by his presence and felt his forgiveness, as people do. They had not expected these experiences, which had come upon them suddenly and vividly, making them think that their teacher was still alive, as people do.

Conceptions of the Afterlife
•   One key difference between modern people living in 21st-century America and the disciples of Jesus living in 1st-century Palestine is

that today, people who believe in the afterlife tend to think that after death, a person's soul goes to heaven even as the body deteriorates. In other words, for most people today, the afterlife is a spiritual experience, occurring after the body is dead.

- But Palestinian Jews, such as the disciples, believed that the afterlife was a physical experience to be lived in the same body that had died once the resurrection took place and people returned to their bodies to enjoy a material eternal life.

- How, then, would those people understand an after-death communication from a deceased loved one?
    o For them, if Jesus was alive again, it was not because his spirit lived on after death. It was because he had been brought back to life in his body.

    o But then where is his body if he comes and goes and is nowhere to be found once the vision is over?

    o For the disciples, there was a clear and obvious answer. Jesus had been raised in the body, and his body had been taken up to heaven. Jesus had been exalted to the realm of God. He had, in fact, been made divine.

Suggested Reading

Bentall, "Hallucinatory Experiences."

Brown, *An Introduction to the New Testament.*

Connell, *Meetings with Mary.*

Ehrman, *How Jesus Became God: The Exaltation of a Jewish Preacher from Galilee.*

Fredriksen, *From Jesus to Christ.*

Goulder, "The Baseless Fabric of a Vision."

Guggenheim and Guggenheim, *Hello from Heaven!*

Harnack, *History of Dogma*.

Laurentin, *The Apparitions of the Blessed Virgin Mary Today*.

Wiebe, *Visions of Jesus*.

Questions to Consider

1. Do you know of anyone (including yourself!) who has had visions of departed loved ones or of important religious figures? What do you make of these visions?

2. This lecture maintains that historians—whether believers or not—can agree that the followers of Jesus had visions of him after his death and that this is what led them to believe he had been raised. Historians who believe Jesus really was physically raised would say that the visions are veridical, and those who do not would say they are nonveridical, but both could agree that these followers experienced visions. Do you agree or not? Why or why not?

Jesus's Exaltation—Earliest Christian Views
Lecture 13

In the previous lecture, we saw that the followers of Jesus who came to believe that he had been raised from the dead naturally concluded that he had been taken up to heaven and was, therefore, made a divine being. In this lecture, we will see that there are still remnants of this view in some of the writings of the New Testament: that Jesus became the Son of God not when he was born or at some time in eternity past but precisely at his Resurrection.

Christian Traditions before the New Testament
- Let's begin with a sketch of the chronology of early Christianity and the writings of the New Testament.
  - Jesus is usually thought to have died around the year 30 C.E.

  - Our first Christian author was not Matthew, Mark, or one of the other Gospel writers. It was the apostle Paul, whose letters were written about 20 to 30 years after Jesus's life, from about 50 to 60 C.E.

  - The Gospel writers produced their accounts of Jesus's life later. Mark, our first Gospel, was probably written around 70 C.E.; Matthew and Luke, around 80 to 85 C.E.; and John, around 90 to 95 C.E.

- In this lecture, we are interested in what the earliest Christians said about Jesus, that is, the Christians living in the years immediately after his death. But if our first Christian writing is not until around 50 C.E.—20 years after Jesus's death—what can we know about what Christians were saying before that?

- Many people think the book of Acts can provide us with that kind of information. But Acts was written after Luke—sometime after 80 to 85 C.E.—and is widely seen by critical historians as being problematic as a source for events that took place 50 or 60 years earlier.

- Is there any way to get a sense of what the earliest Christians said? The answer is yes. The earliest Christian views can be found in what scholars have called *pre-literary traditions*.

Pre-Literary Traditions
- Pre-literary traditions are brief passages that are quoted by later authors. Because these passages are quotations, it follows that they existed before they were quoted; thus, they are pre-literary.

- These traditions can be recognized by means of careful analyses of New Testament writings. For example, they are embedded in the writings of Paul and the Gospels.

In the letter to the Romans, Paul seems to quote a creed from an earlier tradition: Jesus was made the Son of God at his Resurrection.

- Pre-literary traditions can be recognized by a number of characteristics, as we can see by looking at a specific example: Romans 1:3–4.
  - Virtually all of Paul's letters were written to communities of Christians that he had converted to the faith in order to help them deal with the various theological questions and behavioral problems they were experiencing.

- o The letter to the Romans is the one exception: It is a letter to a church that Paul did not establish. Paul wrote the letter because he wanted to continue his missionary work to the far west, in Spain, and he wanted to solicit the support of the Romans.

- Paul begins the letter by introducing himself and then—it appears—by quoting an old creed that was familiar to both him and the Romans.

- There are clear reasons for thinking that Paul is quoting a pre-literary tradition here.
  - o The quotation is a self-contained unit.

  - o It is highly structured, with poetic-like stanzas (two stanzas with three lines each).

  - o It contains words and phrases not found elsewhere in Paul's writings, such as "seed of David" and "Spirit of Holiness."

  - o And it expresses theological views that are different from what Paul sets forth elsewhere in his writings, for example, that Christ became the Son of God at the Resurrection.

- These all are clues for pre-literary traditions in other passages of the New Testament, as well.

- The teaching of this short creedal statement is clear: Jesus was a man who was made the Son of God at his Resurrection.

Exaltation Christology
- Sometimes, the kind of theology advanced in this passage is called an *adoptionistic Christology*—God adopts the man Jesus to be his Son—or *low Christology*—because Christ is thought to have started out "down on earth" with other humans. But it may be better to consider it an *exaltation Christology*.

- Interestingly, the same basic Christological view can be found in other pre-literary traditions of the New Testament.

- o For example, the book of Acts describes the missionary activities of Jesus's followers after his death. It records numerous speeches, and it is clear that the speeches were written not by the apostles who allegedly delivered them but by the author of Acts himself. This was the general practice of ancient historians, as Thucydides tells us.

- o This is also clearly the case with Luke; the speeches of the illiterate, Aramaic-speaking fisherman Peter sound exactly like the speeches of the highly educated, Greek-speaking intellectual Paul.

- o Even though Luke himself wrote the speeches, he did so sometimes by incorporating earlier traditions. These, then, would be pre-literary traditions. And strikingly, these also contain remnants of exaltation Christologies.

- Acts 13:33 is a clear example of an exaltation Christology: God made Jesus his Son by raising him from the dead. The same is true of Acts 2:36. Here again, Jesus is made the Lord at his Resurrection.

Jesus as Adopted Son
- When it comes to evaluating these exaltation Christologies, it is important to stress that they are not saying lowly things about Jesus. Instead, they exalt Jesus in remarkable and magnificent ways: He was taken up to be with God and has been made a divine being.

- The best way to understand such a Christology is by understanding it in relationship to practices of adoption in the Roman world, as shown in the 2011 book by Michael Peppard, *The Son of God in the Roman World*.
  - o It was not uncommon for a Roman aristocratic man to "adopt" another younger man as a son. This gave the adopted son the inheritance rights to his new father. The adopted son had all the privileges, prestige, wealth, and power of his adopted father.

- o Adopted sons were generally considered to be superior to natural sons. Natural sons were who they were simply by chance of birth; adopted sons earned their way into favor by their remarkable qualities.

- o The difference between a natural son and an adopted son can be seen in the case of Julius Caesar: His natural son (born to Cleopatra) was Caesareon, who is a mere footnote in history; his adopted son was Octavius, later known as Caesar Augustus. There is no question about which of the two sons received the prestige, wealth, and power of his father.

- To say that Jesus was the adopted Son of God was an incredibly exalted thing to say about him. By being adopted, Jesus became heir to all of God's power and glory.

- Recall that in the Greco-Roman world, there were three ways for a human to be divine; this is the first of those ways—a human exalted to the level of divinity. The Romans said that this happened to Romulus and to many others; Christians said that it happened to Jesus.

- But later Christologies would move on to say even more exalted things about Jesus, as we will see in the following lectures.

Suggested Reading

Brown, *An Introduction to the New Testament*.

Casey, *From Jewish Prophet to Gentile God*.

Dunn, *Christology in the Making*.

Ehrman, *How Jesus Became God: The Exaltation of a Jewish Preacher from Galilee*.

Fredriksen, *From Jesus to Christ*.

Garrett, *No Ordinary Angel*.

Gieschen, *Angelomorphic Christology*.

Harnack, *History of Dogma.*

Hengel, *Between Jesus and Paul.*

———, *The Son of God.*

Hurtado, *Lord Jesus Christ.*

———, *One God, One Lord.*

Peppard, *The Son of God in the Roman World.*

Questions to Consider

1. Does it seem plausible to you that scholars can isolate pre-literary traditions in the New Testament that can reveal what Christians were thinking before the books of the New Testament were written?

2. What do the exaltation views of the pre-literary traditions found in the books of Romans and Acts tell us about the earliest Christian beliefs about Jesus?

The Backward Movement of Christology
Lecture 14

In the previous two lectures, we saw that the earliest Christians believed that by raising Jesus from the dead, God made him into a divine being. In this lecture and the ones that follow, we will see that over time, Christians came to consider this earliest Christological view inadequate, and they began pushing the Christological "moment"—the point at which Jesus was thought to have become divine—further back in history. Ultimately, they came to believe that Jesus had never ever been "made" the Son of God but had always been the Son of God—equal with God from the very beginning. In this lecture, we will begin to trace that development.

Authors of the Gospels

- As we've said, scholars are virtually unified in thinking that Mark was the first Gospel, written around 70 C.E.; Matthew and Luke were written 10 or 15 years later, around 80 to 85 C.E.; and John was last, written around 90 to 95 C.E.

- We continue to call these Gospels Matthew, Mark, Luke, and John, but the reality is that we don't know who wrote them. The books are anonymous; the titles that ascribe them to two of Jesus's disciples (Matthew and John) and to two of the intimate companions of the apostles (Mark and Luke) were added later by scribes copying these books.

- The first author on record to say that these were the persons who wrote the books was a church father named Irenaeus around 180 C.E. For many decades, then, the books had circulated anonymously.

- Scholars are in wide agreement that the books were not written by any of Jesus's own followers, who were illiterate, Aramaic-speaking Jews from rural Palestine; these books were written by highly educated, Greek-speaking Christians from outside of Palestine.

- Where these authors got their information about Jesus is a complicated question. But it is almost certainly the case that they inherited their stories from earlier traditions—possibly written and certainly oral. People told stories about Jesus for years until Mark wrote them down, then Matthew and Luke, and then John. It does not take much imagination to realize what happens to stories that are passed along in the oral tradition: They are changed and even invented.

- These are the stories that the Gospel writers inherited. We can expect, then, that these stories will have different points of view depending on who told them, under what circumstances, for what purposes, and when.

- As the stories of Jesus changed over the decades, so, too, did the views of who he was. Christians from the very beginning had a remarkably exalted view of Christ as the one adopted by God to be his Son at his baptism. But as time went on, they began to say even more exalted things about Jesus.

Christological Progression
- One of the great New Testament scholars of the second half of the 20th century was Raymond Brown, who sometimes talked about the "backward movement" of Christology.
  - The first Christians said that Jesus was made the Son of God at the Resurrection.

  - Later Christians maintained that he had been the Son of God for his entire ministry; thus, he was adopted by God at his baptism.

  - Still later Christians came to think that he had been the Son of God for his entire life; thus, he was actually born the Son of God.

  - And still later Christians insisted that Christ had been the Son of God before he came into the world, that he had always been the Son of God and had existed with God from the very beginning.

- We can find all four of these views in the New Testament.
  - The idea that Jesus became the Son of God at the Resurrection is in our oldest pre-literary traditions.

  - The idea that he became the Son of God at his baptism is in the oldest Gospel, Mark.

  - The idea that he was born the Son of God is in the next two Gospels to be written, Matthew and Luke.

  - And the idea that he had always been the Son of God from eternity past is in the last of the Gospels to be written, John.

- As we have seen, the first three Gospels—Matthew, Mark, and Luke—are called the Synoptic Gospels because they are alike in many ways. But they also have differences among themselves, including with respect to their understanding that Christ is the Son of God.

Christology in Mark
- Mark, the earliest Gospel, appears to understand that Jesus was adopted to be the Son of God not at his Resurrection but at the baptism.

- In this Gospel, there is no narration of Jesus's miraculous birth from a virgin and no hint that the author knows anything about a virgin birth.

- The Gospel begins with Jesus as an adult, in the account of his baptism by John. It is at this baptism that God declares Jesus to be his Son (Mark 1:11), with the Spirit coming upon him to anoint him.

- It is only at that point that Jesus begins to perform miracles and deliver remarkable teachings. Why did he not do so earlier? Because now, since the baptism, he has been made the Son of God.

- As the Son of God, Jesus is obviously related to God and is, in some sense, himself divine, that is, a superhuman being whose ultimate home is with God in heaven. But Jesus is clearly not the one true God himself.

- It is interesting that virtually no one recognizes Jesus as the Son of God in the Gospel of Mark.
  - That is true of the people he grew up with before God made him his Son (Mark 6), and it is true even of his mother and siblings (Mark 3).

  - With no virgin birth narrative, there is no reason that Mary should realize Jesus is different from everyone else.

The understanding of Mark, our earliest Gospel writer, seems to be that Jesus became the Son of God at his baptism.

- In the Gospel of Mark, there is nothing to suggest that Jesus's birth and upbringing were in any way unusual. That view was to change in the later Gospels.

Christology in Matthew and Luke
- Matthew and Luke both used Mark as a source for their accounts of Jesus's life, but they also had other traditions at their disposal, including accounts of Jesus's unique and highly significant birth to

a virgin. In these accounts, Jesus does not become the Son of God at his baptism but at his conception.

- This can be seen most clearly in the Gospel of Luke, which alone has the story of the Annunciation to Mary. Here, the angel Gabriel tells Mary that she will conceive by the Holy Spirit; thus, the one born of her will be called the Son of God (Luke 1:35).
  - o The earlier exaltation views of the pre-literary traditions and of Mark were comparable to the stories in pagan and Jewish circles of humans being made divine, for example, at their deaths.

  - o This view in Luke is comparable to the second way that a person in antiquity could be divine—by being born to the union of a god with a mortal. The key difference here is that in Luke, Mary does not actually have sex with God but is somehow made pregnant by his Spirit.

- The Gospel of Matthew also has an account of Jesus's being born of a virgin.
  - o Here, we are told that the reason Jesus was to be born of a virgin is that this is what is predicted in Scripture (Matthew 1:22–23).

  - o In reality, the passage of Scripture that Matthew is quoting here (Isaiah 7:14) does not say that the woman who bears a son will be a virgin and is probably not making a prediction of a future messiah figure. Matthew had a different interpretation of the passage because he was reading it not in the original Hebrew but in Greek.

  - o This is part of Matthew's attempt to show that everything about Jesus fulfilled Scripture, including his birth in Bethlehem, the slaughter of the innocents in Bethlehem, his flight to Egypt, and so on.

o   Behind it all, however, appears to be a tradition that Jesus was born of a virgin because it was at that point that he came to be the Son of God.

Christ as Preexistent

- It is important to note that in none of these traditions is there any word to indicate that Jesus preexisted his birth.

- In Mark, there is not even a hint that Jesus's mother was a virgin: She doesn't even know who he is, which is why she and his brothers try to take him out of the public eye—they think he's gone out of his mind.

- In Matthew and Luke, Jesus's mother is a virgin, which is why the story about Mary and the brothers trying to take Jesus away has been omitted from these Gospels.

- But in Matthew and Luke, the moment of the virgin birth is not the time that a preexistent divine being came into human flesh. For Matthew and Luke, Jesus's conception by a virgin made pregnant by God is the point at which he came into existence.

- Only later Christians came up with the idea that Christ was a preexistent God who became flesh through the Virgin Mary. They came to that view by accepting what Matthew and Luke said about Jesus's virgin birth and what John says: that Christ was a preexistent divine being. Note that John does not have a virgin birth.

- In other words, the later classic doctrine of the incarnation through the Virgin Mary was created by combining the views of Matthew and Luke, on the one hand, and John, on the other, creating a view that precisely none of the Gospels themselves has.

- We will soon get to John's unique understanding of Christ. But first, it is important to look at the views of the apostle Paul, who represents a kind of bridge or transition figure between the earlier exaltation Christologies and the later incarnation Christologies.

Suggested Reading

Brown, *An Introduction to the New Testament*.

——, *The Virginal Conception and Bodily Resurrection of Jesus*.

Casey, *From Jewish Prophet to Gentile God*.

Dunn, *Christology in the Making*.

Ehrman, *How Jesus Became God: The Exaltation of a Jewish Preacher from Galilee*.

Fredriksen, *From Jesus to Christ*.

Harnack, *History of Dogma*.

Hurtado, *Lord Jesus Christ*.

——, *One God, One Lord*.

Peppard, *The Son of God in the Roman World*.

Questions to Consider

1. What is the evidence that Mark understands that Jesus "became" the Son of God at his baptism, rather than, say, at his Resurrection?

2. How does Luke's virgin birth story radically change Mark's understanding of what it meant for Jesus to be the Son of God?

Paul's View—Christ's Elevated Divinity
Lecture 15

Next to Jesus, the apostle Paul is the most important figure in early Christianity. There are more books in the New Testament attributed to Paul than to anyone else—more than half of the New Testament is directly or indirectly by or about him. And more than anyone else, Paul developed the theology of the early church; in particular, he stressed that it was the death and Resurrection of Jesus that brought about a right standing before God and that this salvation came to all people, whether they kept the Law of the Jews or not. Moreover, it was the missionary endeavors of Paul that led to the early growth of the Christian church.

Paul's Conversion

- We know some important facts about Paul's biography from his own writings and from a careful and judicious reading of the book of Acts, largely written about him by a follower of his from the next generation.

- Paul began life as a deeply religious and committed Jew. When he first heard Christians claim that Jesus was the Son of God and the messiah, he thought these claims were blasphemous. A crucified criminal could not be the messiah, let alone a divine being. Because of his opposition to Christian claims about Jesus, Paul became an active persecutor of the church.

- But Paul had one of the greatest conversions in all of history. On the basis of a vision he had of Jesus, probably two to three years after the Crucifixion, he became convinced that Jesus was still alive and that he had, therefore, been raised from the dead.

- That belief changed everything for Paul, and he began to think that if Jesus had been exalted by God at his Resurrection, his death must have been planned by God from the beginning. Thus, Paul came to accept the idea that it was the death of Jesus that could bring salvation from sins. He developed this view more strenuously than any of his Christian predecessors. Salvation came not by the Law of the Jews, not by the sacrifices in the Temple of the Jews, but by the sacrificial death of God's own messiah.

- While Paul reflected on the significance of Jesus's death and Resurrection, he also reflected on the character of Jesus himself—who he really was. And he came up with a view that was different from the exaltation Christologies we have seen so far.

Paul experienced a dramatic conversion after he had a vision of Jesus; he came to believe that the death of Jesus could bring salvation from sins.

Incarnation Christology

- In the Christologies we have looked at, Jesus became the Son of God at some point in his existence—at his Resurrection, his baptism, or his conception.

- It would be a mistake to think that these views developed in a strictly chronological fashion, that is, that all Christians at one point focused on the Resurrection, then they all focused on the baptism, and then on the birth.

  o Different communities had different views of the crucial moment of Jesus's existence at the same time.

  o And yet other Christian communities had still other views, in which there never was a point at which Jesus became the Son of God. In these views, Jesus had been the Son of God even before he came into the world.

- This view is what we might call *incarnation Christology.*
    o The word *incarnation* means "in the flesh" or "becoming flesh." In incarnation Christologies, Jesus is understood to have been a preexistent divine being who became human after living, originally, in heaven with God.

    o In this view, God does not make Christ divine after he was human; he was divine before becoming human. He is not exalted to become the Son of God; he already preexisted his birth as the Son of God.

    o This view corresponds to the third way a human could be divine in the ancient world: Sometimes gods themselves became human.

    o This is the view of Christ found in the writings of the apostle Paul—as we will see, with a twist.

Paul's Letters
- We know about Paul's views because he wrote letters to the churches he established, and we have some of these letters

- There are 13 letters in the New Testament that go under Paul's name, although scholars debate whether Paul wrote all of them.

- The standard view among critical scholars is that he wrote seven of the letters. These are our earliest Christian writings, produced before the New Testament Gospels.

Letter to the Galatians
- One of the most striking passages in Paul is one that lay readers and scholars alike generally pass over without recognizing its significance for ascertaining Paul's view of Christ. This is Galatians 4:14.

- This verse indicates that Paul thinks Jesus was an angel. The Greek grammar of the verse makes this clear: Paul is not saying that the Galatians welcomed him as an angel or, even more, as Christ; he is saying that they welcomed him as an angel, such as Christ.

- This becomes clear when we look at how Paul uses the same kind of grammatical phrase elsewhere, as in 1 Corinthians 3:1, which is unambiguous.

- Paul understands that before Christ came into the world, he was a great angel or, rather, the Angel of the Lord.

- We saw in an earlier lecture that in the Jewish tradition, the Angel of the Lord appeared to such Old Testament figures as Hagar, Abraham, and Moses; he appeared in human form even though he was a divine being; and even though he was called the Angel of the Lord, he was also identified as the Lord himself.

- For Paul, Jesus is that being. The Angel of the Lord has become a human for more than a short few minutes but for an entire lifetime. Jesus is the incarnation of the Angel of the Lord.

- That is why Paul elsewhere can speak of Christ as a preexistent divine being, that is, as a divinity who existed before becoming a human, as seen, for example, in 1 Corinthians 10:4.

Letter to the Philippians

- Paul's Christological views can be seen most clearly in the "Christ poem" that is found in Philippians 2:6–11.

- Scholars widely agree that this poem is a pre-Pauline tradition; in other words, Paul is quoting a hymn or a poem that was in circulation before he wrote the book of Philippians. Whether the poem was written by Paul or someone else is difficult to say, but it is clear that the poem is well structured and well balanced.
    o The first half talks about Christ as a preexistent divine being who humbles himself to become a human.

o   The second half talks about God's rewarding of Christ by exalting him even higher than he was before.

- Several key phrases in the poem help us make sense of its understanding of Christ's identity.
  o   Christ was in the "form of God"—like an angel, who is a divine-like being. But he was not yet equal with God. This is a key point.

  o   In the passage that says equality was not something to be grasped, the Greek word does not seem to mean that there was something that Jesus may have wanted that he didn't grasp after in order to get.

  o   Further evidence of that interpretation is what happens to Christ after he dies. God "more highly" exalts him. This appears to mean that God exalted Jesus "more highly" than he was exalted before by making him equal with God. If he had been "equal" with God before this, he could not be more "highly" exalted at all because there is nothing higher than God!

  o   What is most striking is the end of the poem, where we find an allusion to Isaiah 45:22–23, an Old Testament passage that indicates that only to Yahweh, the God of Israel, would every knee bow and every tongue confess. Now it is to Jesus that every knee shall bow and every tongue confess. Christ has been made equal with God and, with God, deserves the worship of all living beings.

- What we have here is a kind of transition Christology that shares features of both an incarnation Christology, in which Christ is a divine being who becomes human, and an exaltation Christology, as we have seen earlier, where Christ becomes divine.
  o   Christ here is definitely a preexistent divine being, the Angel of the Lord, who becomes human.

○ But he also is exalted at his Resurrection. This exaltation, however, is not like the exaltation we saw in other early Christian traditions. Here, Jesus is not made divine. He is made more divine.

○ But how can a divine being be made "more" divine? In our way of understanding the human and divine realms, divinity can't work that way. God is God; mortals are mortals; and there is a vast gap between the two.

○ But as we have repeatedly seen, that was not the understanding in antiquity. The divine realm was inhabited with all sorts of beings at many levels of power. One could move up the chain or down the chain to become more like the ultimate divine being—the one true God—or less like him.

○ Here, in this poem quoted by Paul, Jesus starts out as a divine being, and as a reward for his humble death on the cross, he is exalted to a level equal with God himself.

• This incarnation Christology then stands against the earlier exaltation Christologies. And as we will see, Christians did not stop here. Eventually, Christians would argue that Jesus was never made more exalted than he started out being in his divine status in heaven before the incarnation; in later views, he was always equal with God, from eternity past.

Suggested Reading

Brown, *An Introduction to the New Testament*.

Casey, *From Jewish Prophet to Gentile God*.

Dunn, *Christology in the Making*.

Ehrman, *How Jesus Became God: The Exaltation of a Jewish Preacher from Galilee*.

Fitzmyer, *Pauline Theology*.

Fredriksen, *From Jesus to Christ*.

Garrett, *No Ordinary Angel*.

Gieschen, *Angelomorphic Christology*.

Harnack, *History of Dogma*.

Hurtado, *Lord Jesus Christ*.

———, *One God, One Lord*.

Segal, *Paul the Convert*.

Questions to Consider

1. What would it mean for Paul to think that Christ was originally an angel?

2. Explain how the poem in Philippians 2:6–11 understands Christ both before his incarnation and after his Resurrection.

John's View—The Word Made Human
Lecture 16

The Gospel of John, the last of the four canonical Gospels, differs from the other three in content, emphases, and theology. As we have seen, the Synoptic Gospels share a number of stories about Jesus, such as his baptism, his parables, and so on. In contrast, John has stories not found in the Synoptics, such as accounts of his miracles. Even more important, John has a much more advanced Christology than the other Gospels. For John, Jesus did not become the Son of God at his baptism, and he was not born the Son of God. In fact, Jesus had always been the Son of God, since time before eternity.

Differences between the Synoptics and John

- The Gospel of John, the last of our four canonical Gospels, differs from the other three in content, emphases, and theology.

- John was probably written at the end of the 1st century, possibly around 90–95 C.E., after the other Gospels and after Paul.
  - o We don't know who the author was; later Christians claimed it was one of Jesus's closest disciples, John the son of Zebedee, an Aramaic-speaking, lower-class fisherman from rural Palestine.

  - o However, the Gospel does not claim to be written by this person; the first writer to assign the Gospel to him was Irenaeus about a century later.

  - o The author is anonymous, and the figure of John is never mentioned in the Gospel.

  - o Moreover, given that John could not read or write (Acts 4:13) and almost certainly did not know Greek, this book was written by someone else—a highly literate, Greek-speaking Christian of a later generation.

- The other three Gospels are called the Synoptic Gospels because they share so much of the same content: stories about Jesus's life, such as the account of his baptism, his exorcisms, his parables, his preaching of the coming kingdom of God, his transfiguration, his institution of the Lord's Supper, his prayer in the Garden of Gethsemane, and his trial before the Jewish authorities, who find him guilty of blasphemy.

In the Synoptic Gospels, Jesus refuses to perform miracles as "signs" of his identity, but in the Gospel of John, he performs a number of miracles, including raising Lazarus from the tomb.

- None of these stories is found in John, which instead has stories not found in the Synoptics, such as the miracle in which Jesus turns water into wine; his healing of a man born blind; his raising of his friend Lazarus from the dead; his conversations with Nicodemus, in which Jesus says that Nicodemus must be born again; and his various "I am" sayings.

- Along with the different contents, John has very different emphases from the other Gospels. In the Synoptics, for example, Jesus refuses to do any miracles as "signs" of his identity so that people can believe in him as the Son of God. In John, Jesus does not refuse to do miraculous signs in order to convince people to believe. On the contrary, in this Gospel, Jesus indicates that he does signs so that people will believe (4:48), and John himself indicates that this is the very purpose of Jesus's miraculous works (20:30–31).

- More than anything, John has a different theology from the other Gospels.
  - The Synoptics, of course, all have their own theological views about Jesus: In Mark, he is the one who becomes the Son of God at his baptism; in Matthew and Luke, he is born the Son of God because his mother is a virgin.

  - In contrast, in John, there is no explicit account of Jesus's baptism, at which a voice comes from heaven to adopt Jesus as God's Son, and there is no story of his virgin birth in Bethlehem.

  - For John, Jesus did not become the Son of God and he was not conceived as the Son of God. Jesus had always been the Son of God—and, in fact, an equal with God—back into eternity.

John's Christological Views
- John's distinctive Christological views can be seen in numerous passages, some of them sayings of Jesus himself, where he is identified as a divine being who existed in glory with God before his coming in the world.
  - In John 8:58, Jesus claims that he is "I am"—the name the Lord God took for himself in the Old Testament when speaking with Moses (Exodus 3). Jesus's Jewish opponents know exactly what he means: They take up stones to execute him for committing blasphemy.

  - In John 10:30, Jesus claims to be equal with God. Once again, his Jewish opponents take up stones.

  - In John 17:5, Jesus claims to have been given magnificent glory with God Almighty in eternity past.

  - In John 20:28, the Gospel climaxes with the confession of doubting Thomas, in which he calls Jesus "my Lord and my God."

o These passages coincide with others in which Jesus uses the term "I am" repeatedly about himself, saying that he is the bread of life; the light of the world; the resurrection and the life; and the way, the truth, and the life. In most instances, he does some kind of miraculous sign to prove that what he says about himself is true.

o All of these sayings are found only in John's Gospel.

• It is important to stress that in none of these saying does Jesus claim to be "identical" with God the Father (to whom he prays, for example), but he is "equal" with him.

• This is obviously a far more exalted Christology than we find in the other Gospels and even in Paul.

John 1:1–18
• The distinctive Christology of John can be seen above all in the Prologue of the Gospel, 1:1–18, which contains one of the "highest" Christological views of the entire New Testament.

• Scholars have long recognized that this is another pre-literary poem.
o The writing style differs from the rest of the Gospel, as seen, for example, in its instances of *staircase parallelism*, where one line builds on the preceding one by repeating its final word.

o Further, the key Christological term is this poem—that Christ is the *Logos*, or "Word," of God—is found nowhere else in the Gospel.

o The author of John took over a poem that he found encapsulated his Christological view, even though the terms it used were somewhat different.

• The poem begins by recalling the very beginning of the Bible: Genesis 1:1.

- Just as God spoke a "word" at the beginning to create the world, so, too, the "Word" was in the beginning as the one through whom God created the world.

- The Word here is a divine hypostasis, as we saw in Lecture 4: a divine characteristic that has taken on its own existence as one that is God—because it is God's own characteristic—yet as one that is separate from God—because it can exist apart from God.

- This Word of God was with God in the very beginning, it was itself God, it created the entire universe, it provides life and light to humans, and it was eventually rejected by those to whom it came.

- This Word, in fact, became a human being: Jesus Christ.
  o It is important to note that in this poem, Jesus did not preexist; the Word did.

  o When the Word became a human, Jesus came into existence.

  o Thus, Jesus is the incarnation of the Word, who came into the world, revealed the truth necessary for salvation, laid down his life for others, and then returned to the Father.

- This view is clearly incarnational and is a step beyond what we found in Paul, who maintained that at the Resurrection, Christ was exalted to a higher position than before. Now, Christ was already a glorified divine being before becoming human.

Similar Views in the New Testament
- Similar views of the exalted preexistent divine Christ can be found in other passages in the New Testament, such as Colossians.
  o Colossians claims to be written by Paul, but it almost certainly was not. As a later book, it has a later Christology.

  o This can be seen especially in Colossians 1:15–16, where Christ is the very "image" of the invisible God; is the one who first came into existence of all creation; and is the one in, through, and for whom all else exists.

- The book of Hebrews appears to have a similar view.
  - o This book was accepted into the Bible by church fathers who thought that Paul wrote it, even though he certainly did not.

  - o It, too, has exalted views of Christ, who is the "heir of all things," is the one through whom the world was made, and is, in fact, called God (Hebrews 1:2, 3, 8).

- We have reached a point where Christians are seeing Christ as a preexistent divine being who is equal with God and who created the entire universe. This is a far cry from the historical Jesus of Nazareth, an apocalyptic preacher who ended up on the wrong side of the law and was executed for crimes against the state. But as we will see, Christians were soon about to say even more exalted things about Christ.

Suggested Reading

Brown, *An Introduction to the New Testament.*

Casey, *From Jewish Prophet to Gentile God.*

Dunn, *Christology in the Making.*

Ehrman, *How Jesus Became God: The Exaltation of a Jewish Preacher from Galilee.*

Fredriksen, *From Jesus to Christ.*

Harnack, *History of Dogma.*

Hurtado, *Lord Jesus Christ.*

———, *One God, One Lord.*

Kysar, *John the Maverick Gospel.*

Smith, *The Theology of John.*

1. In what ways is John different from the other Gospels, especially in its understanding of Christ?

2. Do you see the incarnation Christology of John as radically different from the exaltation Christologies of the earliest Christians, as seen in the pre-literary traditions of the books of Romans and Acts?

Was Christ Human? The Docetic View
Lecture 17

U p to this point of our course, we have restricted our attention to the 1st century C.E. These are the critical years that saw the life and death of Jesus, the beginnings of the belief in his Resurrection, and the writing of most of the books of the New Testament. In this lecture, we begin to move forward in time, beyond the New Testament period, to the 2nd and 3rd centuries, when the Christian movement became even more strikingly diverse. As we will see, different Christian groups, each claiming allegiance to Jesus and his apostles, all adhered to radically different beliefs and practices.

Disputes in Early Christianity
- Christianity was anything but a unified religion in the decades and centuries following the New Testament period.

- There were disputes about how many Gods existed, whether the true God had created the world, and whether the Jewish Scriptures were given by that God. There were disagreements over the importance of Christ's death or even if Christ had actually died. Some Christians claimed that there was only one God, but others said that there were 2, 12, 30, or 365.

- We might wonder why these different groups proclaiming different beliefs didn't simply look in their New Testaments to see that they were wrong.
  - The reason is quite simple: The New Testament as a collection of sacred books did not yet exist, even though the books that were to become the New Testament had already been written.

  - But so, too, had a large number of other books that also claimed to be written by apostles of Jesus.

- o Different groups of Christians appealed to different apostolic books to justify their beliefs.

- • Only one of these groups won the debates over what to believe and which books to consider Scripture. The other groups were eventually marginalized and hounded out of existence.

Docetism
- • One early group maintained that Jesus was so fully divine that he could not have been human. Scholars have called these Christians docetists. The word *docetism* comes from the Greek term *dokeo*, meaning "to seem" or "to appear."
  - o Docetists maintained that because Christ was himself God, he could not really be human; he only "seemed" to be.

  - o One implication was that he did not really die but only "appeared" to do so.

- • This view can be seen as a natural outgrowth of incarnation Christologies, such as can be found in the writings of Paul or John.
  - o Paul, for example, talked about Christ coming in the "likeness" of sinful flesh (Romans 8:3).

  - o And John's Jesus is so divine that even modern interpreters wonder if he can be seen as fully human.

  - o What would happen if the incarnational Christology of John's Gospel was elevated even higher?

- • We get a sense of the answer to this question in a later writing, the book of 1 John, which is also in the New Testament.
  - o This book is a kind of open letter to a community or a theological treatise sent to a community—one that appears to have held the Gospel of John as an authority.

  - o But the author tells us that some members, whom he calls antichrists, have left the community (1 John 2:18–19).

○ Elsewhere, the author indicates what these antichrists believe: Jesus did not actually come to the world in real flesh (1 John 4:2–3). This view is strictly forbidden by the author.

○ That is why he begins his writing as he does, stressing the tactile, real, fleshly character of Christ.

Saint Ignatius
- Such views came to be more pronounced among some Christians living several decades later, as seen in the letters of Ignatius.

- Ignatius is one of the most interesting Christian figures from the early 2nd century, just after the writings of the New Testament.
  ○ He was a bishop of Antioch who was condemned for his Christian beliefs in 110 C.E. and sent to Rome to be thrown to the wild beasts as a martyr.

  ○ En route, he wrote seven letters that still survive. In them, among other things, he warns against false believers who adhere to dangerous teachings about Christ.

- In several of Ignatius's letters he warns against those who have a docetic Christology.
  ○ In his letter to the Trallians, he attacks "atheists" and "unbelievers" who claim that Jesus only appeared to suffer (Trallians 9–10).

  ○ In his letter to the Smyrneans, he also stresses that Christter

In his letters, Ignatius of Antioch attempted to warn against a docetic Christology—the idea that Christ only appeared to be human and to suffer.

truly did suffer, and after his Resurrection, he continued to be a fleshly being (Smyrneans 2–3).

- o   One can see why Ignatius would be so disturbed: If Jesus only appeared to suffer, why should he, Ignatius, have to face the wild beasts in reality?

Marcion

- The most well-known docetist of the early church was a philosopher-teacher known as Marcion, who lived in the middle of the 2nd century

- Marcion was often portrayed as the arch-heretic of ancient Christianity, in no small measure because his views had such enormous success.

- Marcion took his cues from the apostle Paul, who differentiated between the Law of Moses and the Gospel of Christ.

- Marcion saw these two not as complementary to each other—with Christ's Gospel being the fulfillment of the Jewish Law—but as completely at odds with each other.

- Because Christ's Gospel, as preached by Paul, was thoroughly different from the Jewish Law, it must have come from a different God.

- Marcion maintained that there were literally two Gods.
  - o   The God of the Jews was the one who created this world, chose Israel to be his people, gave them his Law, and then condemned them—and all others—for not following it.

  - o   But there was also the God of Jesus, who came into the world to save people from the wrath of the Old Testament God.

- In this understanding, Jesus could not actually have been born into this world as a creature; that would make him subservient to the creator God.

- Thus, Jesus appeared from heaven as if a human being, to bring deliverance from the creator God by seeming to die on a cross. But it was all an appearance.

Summing Up Docetism
- It is easy to see the attraction of these docetic views.
  o Jesus really is fully God.

  o If he really is God, then he obviously cannot, at the same time, be human.

  o He must then merely seem to be human.

- This view ended up losing in the debates over who Jesus was, in no small measure because it came more widely to be believed that if Jesus was not a human, he could not die for human sins; if he did not shed real blood, he could not really have been sacrificed for the sake of salvation; if he did not actually die and rise from the dead, then the religion itself is only an appearance, not a reality.

- Thus, as popular as the docetists were in their own day and as attractive as they might seem even to Christians today, they lost the battle over what Christians ought to believe.

Suggested Reading

Bauer, *Orthodoxy and Heresy in Earliest Christianity*.

Casey, *From Jewish Prophet to Gentile God*.

Ehrman, *How Jesus Became God: The Exaltation of a Jewish Preacher from Galilee*.

———, *Lost Christianities*.

Grant, *Jesus after the Gospels*.

Harnack, *History of Dogma*.

Harnack, *Marcion*.

Hurtado, *Lord Jesus Christ*.

———, *One God, One Lord*.

Kelly, *Early Christian Doctrines*.

Norris, *The Christological Controversy*.

Osborn, *The Emergence of Christian Theology*.

Pelikan, *The Christian Tradition*.

Tobin, "Logos."

Questions to Consider

1. Why would docetists claim that Jesus was not actually a human being? Do you see remnants of that view among any Christian believers you know (or know about) today?

2. Explain why Marcion's theology may have been attractive to so many Christians of his day.

The Divided Christ of the Separationists
Lecture 18

A mong the early groups of Christians, none seemed more dangerous to orthodoxy than the various groups of Gnostics. Gnosticism is difficult to define, but it basically insisted that this material world is a place of misery and suffering that must be escaped by the divine spirits entrapped here in human bodies; escape comes by learning the secret knowledge that the divine Christ brings from above. In this view, Christ is one of the many gods of the upper realm; he temporarily inhabited the body of the man Jesus during his ministry to deliver his message of saving knowledge.

Defining *Gnosticism*

- Among the groups of early Christians that were widely seen as among the most dangerous heretics were various groups of Gnostics.

- *Gnosticism* is an umbrella term for a range of Christian groups that shared a number of features.

- They are called Gnostic from the Greek word *gnosis* ("knowledge") because these groups emphasized the importance of secret knowledge for salvation.

- For these groups, it was not the death and Resurrection of Jesus that brought about salvation but, instead, the secret knowledge that .Jesus conveyed.

- This was not simply intellectual knowledge of facts; it was more like a kind of personal knowledge or acknowledgment of certain truths as being true for the individual.
  o The saving knowledge involved a realization of who one really was—a person embodying an element of the divine.

- o People must know who they are, where they came from, how they got here, and how they could return to an original state. Jesus is the one who provides that knowledge.

Sources on Gnosticism
- For centuries, scholars gleaned information on Gnosticism from what the enemies of Gnostics among the church fathers said about them.

  - o For example, Irenaeus, bishop in Gaul around 180 C.E., wrote a five-volume work, *Against Heresies*, to counteract the views of different Gnostic groups.

For centuries, scholars drew their knowledge of Gnosticism from writings against it, such as the work of Irenaeus, a bishop in Gaul.

  - o An author named Tertullian, famous as an apologist for Christianity and as a polemicist against forms of Christianity that he disdained, wrote several treatises opposing Gnostics around 200 C.E.

  - o The problem with such sources is that we can never trust our enemies to present our views fairly, assuming that they even understand our views.

- For that reason, we are incredibly lucky that a number of Gnostic writings—written by Gnostics, for Gnostics, and presupposing a Gnostic point of view—were discovered in modern times. No discovery has proved more significant than one that turned up by complete serendipity in 1945.

o In that year, a small group of farmhands, digging for fertilizer in a remote area outside of Nag Hammadi, Egypt, accidentally uncovered a jar that contained 13 leather-bound books.

o Eventually, the books were sold to antiquities dealers and made their way to a museum in Egypt, where scholars learned of their existence and came to study them.

o The books were written on papyrus in the 4th Christian century. But the writings they contain were produced much earlier, most of them probably in the 2nd century.

o Altogether, there are 52 writings found in these books, but some of these are duplicates; thus, there is a total of 46 different works—most of them Gnostic.

• Based on these kinds of discoveries, in conjunction with the writings of opponents who attacked Gnostic religions, we are able to say some things about what various Gnostic groups believed.

o The basic view held by Gnostics is that this material world we live in is not the creation of the one true God but, instead, is a kind of cosmic disaster that needs to be escaped by the divine spirits that are entrapped here in human bodies. Escape comes by realizing one's true identity, the truth about this world, and the truth about the divine realm. This saving knowledge comes from the divine Christ, who comes from above to deliver the truth that can set us free.

o This summary may make Gnostics sound a lot like Marcion, but they were radically different. As we will see, they did not believe in just two gods but in many gods, and unlike Marcion, they believed the problem of existence is that we come from a different world, are trapped here in our bodies, and need to escape—not by faith in Christ but by coming to know the secrets that can set us free.

Gnostic Myths

- The Gnostic texts we have frequently convey these ideas by telling myths to explain how the divine realm came into existence, how the world came to be created, and how elements of the divine came to be entrapped here.

- In most of these Gnostic myths, there originally was one purely spiritual divine being, an unknown and unknowable God.

- From this one, there emanated other divine beings, other gods who inhabited the divine realm. These gods, sometimes called *aeons*, had both familiar and unfamiliar names, for example, Spirit, Christ, and Wisdom, along with the Self-Originate one, Barbelo, and Saklas.

- In many of the systems, the *aeon* Wisdom plays an important role; for some reason, she came to be separated from the divine realm and gave birth to other deities outside that perfect world of divinity. These lesser divine beings were malformed, ignorant, and sometimes evil.

- One of them, often called Ialdabaoth, was the one who created the material world and wrongly declared that he alone was God. In other words, this lower and ignorant divinity was the God of the Old Testament, the God of the Jews, the God of creation.

- He and his minions managed somehow to capture elements of the divine and trap them in this world in human bodies. The goal of the Gnostic religions is to set that spark of the divine free.

- This happens when the truth of the divine realm, this world, and the entrapment of sparks becomes known. And the truth is revealed by a divine *aeon* who comes down temporarily to inhabit a human body in order to teach the secret knowledge that can bring deliverance.

- Gnostics believed that the divine Christ came into Jesus at his baptism in order to reveal the knowledge necessary for salvation;

he then left Jesus at the point at which he was crucified because the divine cannot suffer.

- In this view, Jesus Christ is two beings: a human body with a divine *aeon* temporarily resident in him. We can call this a separationist Christology because it separates the divine from the human in Christ and claims that they are, in fact, two separate entities.

The Coptic Apocalypse of Peter

- This kind of separationist Christology can be seen with particular clarity in one of the most intriguing of the treatises discovered at Nag Hammadi, the Coptic Apocalypse of Peter.

- This book records an apocalypse or a revelation, allegedly given to Peter and written in the first person.

- While Peter is standing on a hill talking with Christ, he sees Jesus down below being arrested and crucified. Then, he sees another Christ above the cross, laughing. Understandably, he is terribly confused, and he asks Christ, with whom he is talking, how all this can be.

- Christ tells him that down below, the shell of the man Jesus is being crucified, but the true, living Christ cannot be harmed; thus, that Christ is above the cross, laughing at those who think they can kill him.

- This, then, is a separationist Christology in which the divine Christ only temporarily inhabits the man Jesus during his ministry to teach the truth of salvation.

- As we will see in our next lecture, these Gnostic separationist views, as well as other "heresies," were eventually stamped out as debates over belief continued and Christians strongly resisted any idea that Christ was two beings instead of one.

Suggested Reading

Bauer, *Orthodoxy and Heresy in Earliest Christianity.*

Brakke, *The Gnostics.*

Casey, *From Jewish Prophet to Gentile God.*

Ehrman, *How Jesus Became God: The Exaltation of a Jewish Preacher from Galilee.*

————, *Lost Christianities.*

Grant, *Jesus after the Gospels.*

Harnack, *History of Dogma.*

Kelly, *Early Christian Doctrines.*

King, *What Is Gnosticism?*

Layton, *The Gnostic Scriptures.*

Norris, *The Christological Controversy.*

Osborn, *The Emergence of Christian Theology.*

Pelikan, *The Christian Tradition.*

Questions to Consider

1. How is a Gnostic understanding of God and the world different from the traditional Christian view?

2. Explain how a separationist Christology works, and why it makes sense within a Gnostic way of looking at the world (and humans and God).

Christ's Dual Nature—Proto-Orthodoxy
Lecture 19

S cholars often refer to the 2nd- and 3rd-century Christians who embraced the views that were later declared orthodox as *proto-orthodox*. The proto-orthodox church fathers insisted on affirming various Scriptures and accepting certain theological views that on the surface appear to be contradictory, leading to highly paradoxical understandings of both Christ and God. Christ was affirmed to be both human and divine at the same time, yet he was seen to be one person, not two. Further, it was affirmed that the Father was God and Christ was God, yet the proto-orthodox insisted there was only one God. In this lecture, we'll look at the development of such paradoxical views.

Defining *Heresy* and *Orthodoxy*
- The term *orthodoxy* comes from two Greek words that literally mean "right belief." *Heresy* comes from a Greek word that literally means "choice."

- Thus, individuals are orthodox if they hold the right belief and are heretics if they choose to hold some other belief.

- If taken in their literal sense, these terms are not useful as historical designations of one Christian group or another.
   o Technically speaking, no one thinks that he or she has chosen to believe something wrong. All people believe that their beliefs are right, which means that everyone is orthodox.

   o Moreover, historians are not able to make judgments about whether one theological view is right or wrong. They can talk only about what different groups happened to believe and which groups ended up with the greatest number of adherents.

   o Thus, historians of early Christianity use these terms simply to refer to the group that won the various theological debates—

calling this group orthodox, whether or not its views were "right"—and the groups that took alternative positions—calling them heretical, whether or not their views were wrong.

Relationship of Orthodoxy and Heresy

- The historical use of the terms correlates with a new understanding of the relationship of orthodoxy and heresy—new at least since the early 20th century.

- The older standard view was promoted by early Christian historians, such as the 4th-century "father of church history," Eusebius.
  - In his 10-volume account of the first 300 years of the Christian faith, Eusebius outlines an understanding of *orthodoxy* (that is, his own understanding of the faith) to have been the original teaching of Jesus and his apostles and the majority view of Christians at all times.

  - For Eusebius, *heresies* were understood to have been corrupted, demon-inspired, minority opinions held by willful and malevolent false teachers.

- That view was turned on its head in 1934 with the work of Walter Bauer.
  - Bauer argued—and tried to demonstrate—that orthodoxy was not the original and majority view of Christianity in the early centuries but was itself was a later development.

  - In Bauer's view, in different parts of Christendom, there were different "original" forms of the faith, and in the battles for converts, only one group won out.

  - This happened to be the group that had a stronghold in Rome, which meant that in the 3rd and 4th centuries, the Roman Catholic Church emerged. *Catholic* means "universal"; thus, this church is the church of Rome that became the church, allegedly, of the entire world.

- Many of the details of Bauer's reconstruction of early orthodoxy and heresy are disputed today, but the basic picture has held up well over the decades since his work.
  - Jesus and his disciples did not teach the views that became central to Christian faith in the 4th century.

  - These views developed over time as Christians thrashed out ways of understanding God, the creation, the Scriptures, Christ, the Spirit, and salvation.

  - One set of views emerged as victorious, and we call the later holders of these views orthodox.

  - But what do we call their predecessors, those who held similar, if somewhat unformed, views in earlier decades and centuries? It has now become customary to call them the *proto-orthodox*.

A Paradoxical Understanding of Christ
- The proto-orthodox church fathers insisted on affirming various scriptural views about Christ that seem to stand at odds with one another.
  - In some passages of the books that later were to become the New Testament, Jesus is discussed as God (for example, in the Gospel of John). In other passages, he is clearly a man (as in Mark). The proto-orthodox insisted he was both.

  - Thus, there arose the paradoxical affirmation that Christ was both man and God at the same time—not half of each but fully each.

- At the same time, the proto-orthodox had to defend themselves against heretical views that emphasized one aspect of what they saw as correct teaching at the expense of another. But the problem is that different so-called heretics—all of whom had to be attacked—made precisely opposite claims.

- That meant that the proto-orthodox attacked views of one heretical group by affirming important views of another group; at the same time, they attacked the views of that second group by affirming views of the first. The result is that heretical views were accepted for what they affirmed but attacked for what they rejected.
  - For example, there were some Christians who continued to hold to the old adoptionistic view that Christ was a full flesh-and-blood human and that he was only "made" divine at his Resurrection. The proto-orthodox agreed that Christ was human but rejected the idea that during his lifetime, he was not also God.

  - Docetists said that Christ was divine but not human. The proto-orthodox agreed that he was divine but rejected the idea that he was not also human.

  - Separationists said that Christ was divine and human because he was two beings. The proto-orthodox agreed that he was divine and human but rejected the idea that he was two persons.

  - The result, again, was a paradoxical Christology: Christ was divine and human at the same time, but he was one person, not two.

A Paradoxical Understanding of God

- This paradoxical understanding of Christ was matched by a paradoxical understanding of God.

- For the proto-orthodox, God was God, but Christ, his Son, was also God. Doesn't that mean there are two gods?

- But for the proto-orthodox, there can't be two gods because Scripture insists there is only one God (Isaiah 45:21).

- Thus, the proto-orthodox insisted that God was God, Christ was God, and the Holy Spirit was God, but there was only one God.

Justin Martyr

- Such paradoxical views can be seen in several prominent proto-orthodox authors of the 2nd and 3rd centuries, including Justin Martyr, who developed earlier views into a more complicated set of reflections on Christ.

- For Justin, Christ was the Angel of the Lord who had occasionally taken on human form in the Hebrew Bible, but he had actually become a full flesh-and-blood human being when he was incarnated as Jesus Christ.

- More than that, Christ was the Word of God who became human and, as such, was simultaneously God and man.

Origen of Alexandria

- In some instances, proto-orthodox thinkers tried to reason beyond the simple paradox. Among these early theologians, none was more brilliant or, eventually, more controversial than Origen of Alexandria.

- Origen was born and raised in Alexandria as a Christian and was an unusually precocious young man, appointed to be head of the school to train converts as a teenager.

- As an adult, he became one of the most prolific authors of all of Christian history, reportedly producing some 2,000 writings.

- Origen was the first Christian ever to attempt to develop some kind of theological system that explained the orthodox understanding of God, Christ, and salvation. We find his system in a book called *On First Principles*, written around 229 C.E.
  - Origen maintained that Christ had existed with God in eternity past as the Wisdom of God and the Word of God. In other words, these hypostases of God were actually Christ himself.

  - But how, if Christ is fully God, as God's own Wisdom and Word, could he become a human without compromising his divinity? And how could he remain divine without compromising his humanity?

o Origen's solution is what eventually led, centuries after his death, to his condemnation as a heretic, even though in his day, he was seen as a leading proponent of orthodoxy. His solution was rooted in his teaching of the "preexistence of souls," that is, the idea that human souls existed before they were born in this world.

o In his view, long ago, God created a large number of souls—intelligent beings—who were to spend their existence contemplating and adoring him through his Word and Wisdom.

o But the souls had free will, and virtually all of them departed from the contemplation of God. As a punishment, God put them into bodies. Those who departed just a little became angels; those who departed a great deal became demons; those in between became humans.

o Only one soul did not stray from contemplating the Word and Wisdom of God. This soul became "one" with Christ in this eternal contemplation, just as a piece of iron placed in a the coals of a hot fire becomes, after a long time, indistinguishable from the fire itself.

o It was this one soul that took on human flesh and became incarnate through the Virgin Mary. Thus, Jesus has a rational soul, like all others humans, yet is completely divine, as one who is completely infused with the Word and Wisdom of God.

• This is a terrifically clever and intelligent attempt to explain how Christ could be both human and divine at the same time.
o It was eventually condemned, though, in part on the grounds that if human souls were lost in the distant past, there seemed to be no guarantee that after they are saved by Christ, they

won't become lost again; that would mean that salvation is only a temporary measure.

o   But for the church fathers, Christ's salvation has permanent, eternal effects. Thus, they had to determine some other way to explain how Jesus Christ was both human and divine. We will see how they did so in the following lectures.

Suggested Reading

Bauer, *Orthodoxy and Heresy in Earliest Christianity*.

Casey, *From Jewish Prophet to Gentile God*.

Dünzel, *A Brief History of the Doctrine of the Trinity in the Early Church*.

Ehrman, *How Jesus Became God: The Exaltation of a Jewish Preacher from Galilee*.

———, *Lost Christianities*.

Eusebius, *The History of the Church*.

Grant, *Jesus after the Gospels*.

Harnack, *History of Dogma*.

Kelly, *Early Christian Doctrines*.

Norris, *The Christological Controversy*.

Osborn, *The Emergence of Christian Theology*.

Pelikan, *The Christian Tradition*.

Rusch, *The Trinitarian Controversy*.

Tobin, "Logos."

1. Explain the contrast between the view of orthodoxy and heresy in Eusebius and in the work of Walter Bauer.

2. Why did the proto-orthodox Christians develop paradoxical understandings of Christ as both God and man at one and the same time?

The Birth of the Trinity
Lecture 20

The Christian doctrine of the Trinity has always been portrayed, by the best theologians, as a mystery. In part, that means that it cannot be completely comprehended or understood with the mind. There are three persons who are all individually God: The Father is God, Christ is God, and the Holy Spirit is God. But there is only one God. In this lecture, we will look at how this teaching came into existence.

The Holy Spirit

- To this point in the course, we have been speaking about God the Father and about how Christ, too, became God. But where did the Holy Spirit come from?

- The Hebrew Bible frequently mentions God's Spirit, which appears to be a being apart from God (Genesis 1:2).

- Christian theologians came to think that the Spirit was a being who was also God but was not the Lord God Almighty, the Father himself.

- Support was found in the words of Jesus about the coming of the Spirit once he left the world (John 14, 16; Acts 2).

- The Spirit, then, was taken to be a third divine being, along with the Father and the Son. But how could they all be divine beings if there was, in fact, only one God? This is the doctrine of the Trinity, in which the three are distinct persons and all of them are God, yet there is only one God.

Development of the Trinity

- It would be a mistake to think that any such view of the Trinity was found in the teachings of Jesus or even in any of the writings of the New Testament. These writings were later used by church fathers in trying to decide how both Christ and God could be God if there is only one God. But nowhere in the New Testament—or even in the first three centuries of the Christian church—is there any direct affirmation of the doctrine of the Trinity, that is, that there are three persons who are all God, yet there is only one God.

The Hebrew Bible seems to describe the Holy Spirit as a being that is separate from God.

- The motivation for the emergence of this Trinitarian idea lies in theological developments at the end of the 2nd and the beginning of the 3rd centuries.
  o At that time, virtually all Christian leaders agreed that there were three beings who were God. But how can one avoid, then, becoming a polytheist—believing in three gods?

  o The most popular solution at the time is a view that scholars have called *modalism*. Its opponents themselves claimed that this was the dominant view among Christians, held even by the bishops of Rome (the early popes) for a time.

- In the modalist view, God has three modes of existence. Just as a single person can be a father, a brother, and a son at the same time, so, too, can God be Father, Son, and Spirit without being three persons.
  o In this view, there is one person in three manifestations or relationships.

o   Support for this view came from scriptural passages emphasizing that there was only one God (Isaiah 44:6) and affirming that Christ was God (Romans 9:5).

o   Christ, then, can't be a separate god from the God of the Old Testament. To think so requires one to believe in two gods. And when the Holy Spirit is added in, that would be belief in three gods. But there is only one.

o   Among the consequences of this view is that it was the Father who came to earth as the Son and was crucified for the sins of the world. Opponents of this view called it *patripassianism*, which means "the Father suffers."

Debates within Proto-Orthodoxy
- One opponent of patripassianism was a church leader in Rome named Hippolytus, who split from the church at large over the issue to be elected by his followers as a kind of rival pope to the ruling pope in Rome.

- Another opponent was Tertullian of Carthage, a feisty antagonist of all things that varied from his particular views, whether pagan, Jewish, or Christian.
    o   Tertullian stressed that there is a difference between being something (say, a husband) and having something (say, a wife). It is impossible to be and to have the same thing at once; that is, one cannot both be and have a wife as one's spouse.

    o   Tertullian also pointed to Scriptures that stressed the difference between the Father and the Son as different beings.

A Divine Economy
- It was a result of this debate that authors started speaking of three different divine beings who made up the one God. Hippolytus called this divine entity the Triad. Tertullian was the first to use the term *Trinity* to describe it.

- Both Hippolytus and Tertullian understood the relationship of Father, Son, and Spirit as a divine "economy."
  - *Economy* in this context does not refer to a monetary system but to a way of organizing relationships.

  - For Tertullian, the three divine beings are in intimate and close relationship with one another, each having his own function but being completely united in substance and power; the three are distinct from one another but not divided.

  - Yet even in this theology—which is far more sophisticated than what one can find in the New Testament or anywhere in the second Christian century—we have not arrived at the final understanding of the Trinity. For Tertullian, the Father is greater than the Son. Later theologians were to argue that they are, in fact, equal.

  - But we are clearly on the way to this later theology, the formation of the doctrine of the Trinity that would become the key paradox and mystery of the Christian faith.

Suggested Reading

Casey, *From Jewish Prophet to Gentile God.*

Dünzel, *A Brief History of the Doctrine of the Trinity in the Early Church.*

Ehrman, *How Jesus Became God: The Exaltation of a Jewish Preacher from Galilee.*

———, *Lost Christianities.*

Eusebius, *The History of the Church.*

Groh and Gregg, *Early Arianism.*

Grant, *Jesus after the Gospels.*

Harnack, *History of Dogma.*

Kelly, *Early Christian Doctrines.*

Norris, *The Christological Controversy*.

Osborn, *The Emergence of Christian Theology*.

Pelikan, *The Christian Tradition*.

Rusch, *The Trinitarian Controversy*.

Questions to Consider

1. Explain a modalist view of Christ and reflect on why such a view may have been attractive to Christian thinkers who wanted to emphasize that Christ is God, yet there is only one God.

2. How did the doctrine of the Trinity emerge out of the debates against the modalists?

The Arian Controversy
Lecture 21

B y the middle of the 3rd century, virtually all Christian leaders agreed with the proto-orthodox paradoxical views about both Christ and God. Christ was understood to be a human being and a divine being at the same time, yet he was only one person, not two. Moreover, the Father was obviously God, Christ was also God, and the Holy Spirit was God, but there was only one God. Sharp divisions arose among Christians involving how to explain these paradoxes in a way that did not compromise one or the other of the affirmations—without denying, for example, that Christ himself was God or without denying that there was only one God.

Novatian

- A good representative of standard proto-orthodox belief in the mid-3rd century was a leader of the Roman church named Novatian.

- Novatian's most famous writing was a treatise on the Trinity. In this writing, he tried to develop an understanding of the Trinity that did full justice to the idea that Christ could be God without being God the Father.

- In other words, Novatian was attacking Christians who said either that Christ was not actually divine himself (such as the early Christian adoptionists, who maintained that Jesus had been elevated to the level of divinity only after his death) or that he was the same being as the Father (the modalists we discussed earlier).
  - o Novatian saw these two heresies as two different attempts to preserve the oneness of God because in neither case is there a "second God" alongside the Father.

  - o But they stressed this point in opposite ways—one by claiming that Christ was not God and the other by claiming he was the Father.

- o In a clever image, Novatian said that Christ was being crucified between these two thieves of heresy. And he wanted to set the record straight.

- In Novatian's view, Christ is truly God; he is distinct from God the Father, yet he is in perfect unity with God.
  - o For Novatian, this does not mean that Christ is equal with God.

  - o If Christ were equal with God; or unborn, as God was; or without a beginning, as God was, that would necessarily mean that there were two gods.

  - o For Novatian, the solution is to think of Christ as a subordinate divinity, who was begotten by the Father before the creation.

- This view was perfectly orthodox in the middle of the 3rd century, but by the opening decades of the 4th century, it would be declared a heinous heresy. This declaration grew out of the Arian controversy.

Arius and Alexander
- The Arian controversy takes its name from the church leader, teacher, and theologian Arius of Alexandria.
  - o Arius was born in Libya around 260 C.E. but moved to Alexandria and ultimately became a leader in the church there.

  - o In 312, he was ordained as a priest and placed in charge of his own church.

  - o His bishop—the ultimate leader of the Alexandrian church— was a man named Alexander.

- The controversy between Arius and Alexander broke out in 318 C.E. Alexander asked the priests who served under him to provide a written interpretation of a certain passage of Scripture, probably Proverbs 8, in which Wisdom is portrayed as a hypostasis of God that exists independently of him and through whom he created the world.

The Arian controversy involved the question of whether God the Father had created the Son or whether the Son existed eternally.

- Arius's interpretation was not to the liking of his bishop.
  - According to Arius, Christ, God's Wisdom, was not himself fully equal with God but was a subordinate deity.

  - For that reason, he had not always existed but had come into being at some point as the first creation of God the Father.

  - It was then through his Son that the Father created the world.

  - But for Arius, only God the Father is without beginning, and he is separated from all other beings, even his Son, by an infinity of glories.

  - The Father and the Son are not comparable. It is the Father who is superior to all things.

- These views were strenuously opposed by Bishop Alexander. In a letter to the bishop of Constantinople, also named Alexander, the bishop of the Alexandrian church explained his views, which he took to be orthodox, against the heresy of Arius.
  - Alexander pointed to Hebrews 1:2, according to which it was through Christ that God had "made the ages." If Christ made the ages, then the ages could not have existed before him; thus, there never was an age when he did not exist. Christ had always existed.

  - Alexander pointed to another passage, Colossians 1:15, in which Christ is said to be the "image of God." If Christ is God's image, he must have always existed because God always has had an image; otherwise, he couldn't exist. Thus, his image—Christ—must have always existed.

  - Moreover, for Alexander, God—because he is God, not a creation—can never change. If God begot Christ at some point of the past, that would mean that God had become a Father, something he was not before. But God could not become something he never was; thus, he must have eternally begotten the Son.

A Rift in the Christian Church

- In response to Arius's public statement of his views, Alexander deposed him from his position as a priest and leader of the church and excommunicated both him and his supporters from the church.

- Arius and those who agreed with him did not go quietly, however. They traveled about the Christian world, explaining the controversy and getting important church leaders to agree with their theological views. The result was a serious rift throughout the Christian church.

- Eventually, the Roman emperor himself—the emperor Constantine—intervened to try to resolve the issues.
  - Constantine was the first Christian emperor, who had converted to the faith in 312 C.E.

o He took an avid interest in church affairs and was dismayed that the followers of Arius and the followers of Alexander could not resolve their theological dispute. Ultimately, he called the Council of Nicea, in the year 325, to settle the issue. We will take a closer look at Constantine in the next lecture.

Suggested Reading

Dünzel, *A Brief History of the Doctrine of the Trinity in the Early Church.*

Ehrman, *How Jesus Became God: The Exaltation of a Jewish Preacher from Galilee.*

Groh and Gregg, *Early Arianism.*

Harnack, *History of Dogma.*

Kelly, *Early Christian Doctrines.*

Osborn, *The Emergence of Christian Theology.*

Pelikan, *The Christian Tradition.*

Rusch, *The Trinitarian Controversy.*

Questions to Consider

1. In what ways are the views of Arius similar to the views we find in such writers as Tertullian and Novatian (as discussed in Lecture 20)?

2. What are the differences between Arius's views of Christ and Alexander's? Why did this issue seem so important to so many people?

The Conversion of Constantine
Lecture 22

The significance of the Council of Nicea and the role that the emperor Constantine played in it cannot be grasped without understanding further the history of the Christian movement in the three centuries leading up to it. Therefore, this lecture will deal with the background to the most unexpected and history-transforming event: when a Roman emperor, rather than persecuting Christians, himself became a Christian and took a leading role in deciding theological issues being debated within the church.

Early Christianity in the Roman Empire

- To make sense of Constantine's conversion, we need to consider a brief history of the relationship of the Christian religion to the Roman Empire.

- As we have seen, the earliest Christians were a group of Jews who came to believe that Jesus had been exalted to heaven when God raised him from the dead.

- These earliest Christians began to seek converts among their fellow Jews. As far as we know, this led to some opposition among non-Christian Jews but no opposition, at least at the outset, from Roman authorities. If they had heard about these conflicts, the authorities would have considered them an internal Jewish affair.

- But eventually, with the missionary efforts of the apostle Paul and others like him, Gentiles began to convert to the Christian faith, believing that Christ had died, had been raised from the dead, and had been exalted to heaven. As the church became increasingly Gentile, it became decreasingly Jewish.

Pagans and Early Christians

- There are three key questions we need to ask and answer about pagans and their relationship to early Christians:

o   Why did pagans worship the gods they did?

o   Why did they persecute Christians for worshipping their own God?

o   What compelled some pagans to convert to the Christian faith—a few at first but, in the end, masses?

- As it turns out, the answer to all three questions is the same. It all has to do with ancient understandings of divine power.

- Pagans, as a rule, worshipped their many gods because the gods were powerful and could provide for humans what humans could not provide for themselves out of their own resources: rain, crops, health, safe childbirth, victory in war, life, peace, happiness, and so on.

- Christians were persecuted not because they considered Jesus God or because they insisted on worshipping him and God the Father, but because they refused to worship the gods who were powerful enough to made life livable, happy, and prosperous for other members of the empire.
  o   If the gods are the ones who make life possible and successful, and all they require are simple, occasional acts of worship, then anyone who refused to worship them must be the cause of disasters, such as droughts, famines, earthquakes, military defeats, and so on.

  o   Because the Christians were the ones who refused to worship the state gods, they were the cause of problems in the community; that is why they were persecuted.

- Divine power also explains why pagans began to convert to worship the Christian God: It was a matter of who was better able to provide what was needed in life. Christians succeeded in convincing pagans that Christ and his Father were more powerful than their gods; that they alone could provide what is needed for this life; and that they could, in fact, provide eternal life. Once they were convinced of this, pagans converted.

- There did not need to be massive conversions between the days of Paul and the days of the emperor Constantine to make Christianity a major player on the religious scene by the early 4th century. Usually, it is estimated that about 5 percent of the empire had converted at that time. If that's the case, then the faith that started out with only a small group of Jesus's followers would have needed to grow about 40 percent every decade during its first 300 years.

  o So far as we know, there were no other religions like Christianity in the ancient world, that is, religions that were both missionary and exclusivistic. Judaism may have been exclusive, but it was not missionary; a number of Greco-Roman religions were missionary, but they were not exclusivistic.

  o Christianity succeeded, in no small part, precisely because it alone among the religions of antiquity insisted on the exclusivity of its views. Because converts needed to renounce their former religions, Christianity destroyed all other religions as it grew.

  o The steady conversions to Christianity often made the pagans' former families and friends even angrier, which meant that persecutions ratcheted up as the church grew in size and importance.

  o We see this kind of animosity reflected already in the New Testament and still later in the remarks of the Christian apologist Tertullian.

Christian Persecutions

- Contrary to what is often imagined, the Roman emperors were rarely involved directly with the persecution of Christians.

- The first time an emperor was involved with a persecution was under Nero (64 C.E.), a persecution that was localized and that was not an attempt to attack Christians for being Christian.

- Similar things could be said about persecutions during the time of Trajan (112 C.E., as seen in the letters of Pliny the Younger) and Marcus Aurelius (177 C.E., as seen in the Letter of Lyons and Vienne).

- The first empire-wide persecution instituted by an emperor did not occur until 249 C.E., under the emperor Decius. Luckily for the Christians, it lasted only for a couple of years, until the death of Decius in 251 C.E.

The emperor Nero tried to shift blame for the great fire in Rome in 64 C.E. from himself to the Christians, thus instituting a localized persecution.

- What is called the Great Persecution occurred under the Roman emperor Diocletian, starting in 303 C.E. Diocletian sought to rid the empire of the growing Christian presence.

Constantine's Conversion

- Just three years later, in 306 C.E., Constantine became the emperor, and six years after that, in 312 C.E., he converted to Christianity.
  - We have an account of his conversion in a biography of Constantine written by Eusebius, who was his contemporary and claimed to have firsthand accounts at his disposal.

  - According to these accounts, Constantine was deeply disturbed on the eve of a significant battle and wondered how he could receive divine assistance for his military cause.

- o Constantine claimed that the night before the battle, he had a dream of the cross and was told in his dream that this was the sign that would give him victory.

- o He had the sign embossed on his soldiers' shields, went into battle, and emerged victorious. From then on, Constantine considered himself a follower of Christ.

- There are disputes over whether this was a "genuine" conversion or not, because there are some signs that Constantine continued to worship other divinities, especially the god of the sun, but it appears that his commitment to the Christian religion was genuine. Most significantly, his actions began to favor the Christians greatly over other religions.

  - o Constantine saw to it that persecutions were put to an end.

  - o He donated large tracts of land to the church and built magnificent churches.

  - o He elevated the status of the clergy significantly.

  - o And he promoted the worship of the God Christ to the state gods.

- Constantine's conversion was significant indeed: Now, the Roman emperor, rather than being a god who was worshipped, was a servant of God who urged his subordinates to worship Christ. Now, rather than being the Son of God in competition with Christ, the emperor became the servant of God in subservience to Christ.

- It is wrong to say that Constantine made Christianity the state religion. That would not happen until the emperor Theodosius at the end of the 4th century. But Constantine certainly made Christianity a favored religion. And by intervening in internal church affairs, such as the Arian controversy, he guaranteed that Christian concerns would be the concerns of the entire empire.

- In the next lecture, we will consider why Constantine may have been so invested in solving this controversy, which on the surface may have seemed simply to involve a rather technical theological point of whether Jesus was a god who came into being before the world or whether he had always existed alongside God the Father.

Suggested Reading

Carroll, *Constantine's Sword.*

Ehrman, *How Jesus Became God: The Exaltation of a Jewish Preacher from Galilee.*

Eusebius, *The History of the Church.*

Groh and Gregg, *Early Arianism.*

Harnack, *History of Dogma.*

Questions to Consider

1. How often and severe were the persecutions of Christians by Roman emperors prior to Constantine?

2. What do you suppose were the leading factors behind the conversion of the emperor Constantine?

The Council of Nicea
Lecture 23

In 325 C.E., the emperor Constantine called a council of bishops from around the world to resolve this question: In what sense was Jesus God? Arius's supporters maintained that Jesus was a subordinate divinity, the creation of God the Father, who came into being at some point in time. Alexander's supporters insisted that Christ never came into being but had always existed and was absolutely equal with God. Constantine was concerned about the issue not because he was theologically invested, but because for the Christian church to achieve his political objectives, he needed it to be unified. In the end, the council overwhelmingly supported Alexander's views over those of Arius, who was declared a heretic.

Agenda of the Council

- Even though the Council of Nicea was the most momentous and important church council in the history of Christianity, its agenda and decisions are widely misunderstood today.

- People often think that the Christian leaders at the council "invented" the New Testament by deciding which Gospels, epistles, and so on would be considered Scripture. But the bishops at the Council of Nicea did not discuss which books should be accepted into the canon.

- People also often think that the Council of Nicea is when Jesus began to be considered God. Sometimes, it is said that a vote was taken at the council, for the first time, over whether or not Jesus was the Son of God and that it was a close vote. Of course, that's not true either.
  - We have already seen that Jesus was considered the Son of God—in fact, himself a divine being—virtually at the outset of the Christian faith, soon after his death, as his own disciples declared that he had been taken up into heaven and exalted to the level of divinity.

o   Jesus is called the Son of God and even God in the writings of the New Testament, and he was considered God by all the proto-orthodox and most of the heretical Christians that we know about in the 2nd and 3rd centuries.

- As we will see, everyone at the Council of Nicea agreed that Jesus was the Son of God—or even God. The only question was: In what sense was he God? Was he a subordinate deity who came into being at some point in the remote past before he created the world, as Arius and his followers said? Or was he fully equal with God and coeternal with him, so that there never was a time when he did not exist, as Bishop Alexander said?

Constantine's Concern

- Even before the council met, the emperor Constantine was concerned about this question, not because he was theologically trained or had any interest in refined points of Christian doctrine. Constantine was concerned because he saw in Christianity a potentially unifying force in his fractured empire.

- The empire was vast and was culturally, politically, and religiously fragmented. In contrast, Christianity emphasized oneness: There is one God, one Son of God, one church, one faith, one hope, and so on. Christianity was a religion of unity. Constantine believed it could be used to unify the empire.

- But the problem was that this religion of unity was itself split; thus, Constantine saw the need to heal the split if the Christian church was to bring real religious unity to the empire.

- Eusebius's biography of the emperor, *The Life of the Blessed Emperor Constantine*, preserves a letter that Constantine himself sent to Arius and Alexander to try to get them to see eye to eye on the theological issue dividing them and their followers. He is quite forthright that his concern is that Christians should be united in their beliefs. Further, he considered the issue at stake to be petty and trivial.

- Constantine had the letter hand-delivered to the two opponents by Ossius, an important bishop of Cordova, Spain.
  - After delivering the letter, Ossius came back by a land route that took him through Antioch, Syria.

  - While there, he attended a conference of church bishops that met to debate the Arian issue and in which Arius and his views were condemned by the majority.

  - The supporters of Arius at this conference were told, however, that they would have a chance to defend their position. Thus, the Council of Nicea was born.

A Worldwide Gathering

- The Council of Nicea was the first of the seven ecumenical councils of the church.

- The term *ecumenical* comes from a Greek word that means "world." These councils were not merely local in nature but were worldwide, meaning that leaders from around the world attended in order to determine what Christian beliefs were to be adhered to by believers everywhere.

- The Council of Nicea was originally scheduled to meet in Ancyra, a city in Asia Minor (modern Turkey), but it was eventually moved to Nicaea, also in Asia Minor.

- The vast majority of the 318 bishops who attended came from the eastern part of the empire: Egypt, Palestine, Syria, Asia Minor, and so on. Western Christians were not well represented; in fact, not even the bishop of Rome, Sylvester, came but sent two legates in his place.

- Still, the decisions of the council were considered binding on all Christians everywhere, in no small part because the emperor himself presided over the council and sanctioned its findings.

The Nicene Creed

- After debating the issues back and forth, the council decided against the views of Arius and his followers.

- It was not, in fact, a close vote. All but 20 bishops agreed with these decisions. And after Constantine himself twisted their arms, 17 of those 20 agreed to sign off on the concluding statement.

- This statement was a creed that expressed the now-orthodox position and anathematized (that is, uttered a divine curse against) anyone who thought differently.

With the Nicene Creed, the Jesus who had been crucified as a common criminal became equal to God himself.

© Hayden Wood/iStock/Thinkstock.

- Several points in the creed are worth emphasizing:
  o Because it was the nature of Christ as God that was the major point of contention, the creed's statements about Christ are far more lengthy, involved, and nuanced than anything said about God the Father or the Holy Spirit.

  o Christ in this creed is not a subordinate deity to God. He is "of one substance" with the Father. The word used here is *homoousios*, a word that would become significant in the later history of debates over Christ's character after the council.

o   According to the creed, Christ is completely equal with God and himself the "true God"; there was never a time when he did not exist.

Christ of the Nicene Creed
- The Christ who emerged from the Council of Nicea is obviously a far cry from the historical Jesus of Nazareth.

- Jesus was an itinerant apocalyptic preacher from the backwaters of rural Galilee, who offended the authorities and was unceremoniously crucified for crimes against the state.

- Now, he was confessed to be God himself, equal with the Father from eternity past. Whatever he may have been in real life, Jesus had now become fully God.

Suggested Reading

Dünzel, *A Brief History of the Doctrine of the Trinity in the Early Church.*

Ehrman, *How Jesus Became God: The Exaltation of a Jewish Preacher from Galilee.*

Eusebius, *The History of the Church.*

Groh and Gregg, *Early Arianism.*

Harnack, *History of Dogma.*

Questions to Consider

1. Why do you think the head of the entire empire, the emperor Constantine, would be interested in or concerned about a theological controversy over whether Christ was coeternal and of the same substance as God the Father?

2. Explain the Christological views set forth in the creed of Nicea.

Once Jesus Became God
Lecture 24

We might think that with the declarations of the Council of Nicea, Jesus was fully, substantially, and eternally God, and that was the end of the story. But of course, every ending marks a new beginning, and the final verdict that Jesus was God had resounding implications and ramifications. In this final lecture, we will consider these implications. They involve Christians in relation to the pagan world, to Jews, and to themselves.

Results of Constantine's Conversion

- The results of Constantine's conversion and his intervention in Christian affairs obviously had an enormous effect on the broader Roman world.

- Now, rather than being a persecuted and relatively small minority within the empire, Christianity began to assert itself as a favored religion, with masses of conversions; by the end of the 4th century, nearly 50 percent of the empire was Christian.

- At that time, in less than 60 years after the Council of Nicea, the Roman emperor Theodosius, a fiercely committed Christian, made Christianity the religion of the state for all practical purposes. It became illegal to engage in pagan activities, such as sacrifices to the pagan gods.

- The emperors were no longer the enemies of Christ and persecutors of his people; they were the worshippers of Christ and patrons of his people.

- From that time on, Christianity was destined to become the religion of the West. This never would have happened had Jesus not come to be considered God.

- o Christianity would have remained a small group of Jewish followers of Jesus who continued to think of him as an important teacher of the Law of Moses, which they would have followed and insisted that other members of their sect follow.

- o Christianity would never have broken out of its Jewish matrix, converted masses of Gentiles, converted the Roman emperor, or become the dominant religion of Western culture and civilization.

- o We never would have had the Middle Ages, Renaissance, Reformation, or arguably, the Enlightenment. That Jesus became God had historical, cultural, social, political, and economic effects that can scarcely be calculated.

Rise of Anti-Semitism

- Some of the effects of Jesus's becoming God were directly related to the Jewish people, most of whom retained their own religion and, of course, refused to acknowledge that Jesus was in any sense God.

- There was nothing in Jesus's earthly proclamations that made him stand out as in any way non-Jewish. He and his followers kept the Jewish Law, followed Jewish customs, and studied the Jewish Scriptures.

- His followers believed, during his life, that he was the Jewish king of the coming kingdom, but they did not think that he was starting a new religion.

- But after his death, these followers came into sharp conflict with other Jews—those who refused to believe that Jesus had been sent by God as a Jewish messiah and who had been raised from the dead as a divine being.

- Jesus's followers maintained that the belief in the death and Resurrection of their messiah was essential for salvation.

- o In their view, Jews who rejected that message rejected their own salvation, which meant that they were alienated from God and doomed for eternal destruction.

- o Non-Christian Jews were soon seen as hard-hearted and rebellious against God.

- o It was not long before Christians began to declare that because Jews had rejected God, God had rejected them.

- o Thus began the long history of Christian anti-Judaism that resulted in the horrific acts of anti-Semitism of our own day and age.

- We can see the beginnings of this history already within the pages of the New Testament, where Jews are often characterized as the opponents of Christ, as hard-hearted sinners against God, and even as children of the devil.

- This kind of polemic against Jews came to more vehement expression in the second Christian century, as can be seen, for example, in a sermon discovered in modern times, delivered by a bishop of the city of Sardis named Melito.
  - o This sermon is an attack on Jews for rejecting the one God had sent to them for their own salvation.

  - o More than that, because Christ was God, Melito believed that Jews, who were responsible for his death, were guilty of murdering God.

  - o His is the first charge of deicide to be recorded against Jews, and it is rooted, of course, in the belief that Jesus himself is actually God.

- It is one thing for a small, persecuted minority to lash out against others with its powerless rhetoric. But what happened when this belief in Jesus as God came to be the religion of the state? What happened when it became the majority opinion and had the power of empire to back it up? The answer is that the rhetoric used earlier to attack Jews verbally was transformed into political power, so that Jews were attacked physically—in state legislation, in imperial mistreatment, and in mob violence.

o   Jews became legally marginalized under Christian emperors and made second-class citizens with restricted legal rights and limited economic possibilities.

o   By the end of the 4th century, it became illegal for a Christian to convert to Judaism, for a Christian to marry a Jew, and for Jews to serve in public office. In 423 C.E., it became illegal for Jews to build or even repair a synagogue.

o   Accompanying these forms of legislation were acts of violence against Jews, such as the burning of synagogues, which even if not sponsored by the state authorities, were tacitly condoned.

•   Once those who believed that Jesus was God were given secular power, they used that power against their long-time enemies, the Jews who rejected the Christ God.

Internal Effects in the Church
•   Along with these external conflicts, the declaration of Jesus as God at the Council of Nicea had an effect on the internal workings of the church, as well, especially as theologians worked to understand the nuances of the faith with greater sophistication.

•   One historical result of the Council of Nicea is not widely known. As it turns out, the condemnation of Arius did not lead to the demise of the Arian party or its views.

o   On the contrary, even though the council condemned Arius, he continued to have enormous influence among Christian leaders and lay people throughout the empire.

o   After Constantine passed from the scene, other emperors preferred the Arian understanding of Christ as a subordinate divinity who came into existence at some point in the distant past.

o   That is why, some 55 years after Nicea, the church father Jerome could complain, "the world groaned and was astonished to find itself Arian."

o   The debates continued until the second ecumenical council, the Council of Constantinople in 381 C.E. At this council, the decisions of Nicea were restated and reaffirmed, and Arianism from that point on became a marginalized minority considered extremely heretical.

- But not even that ended the disputes over theology. Even when all major Christian thinkers accepted the affirmations of Nicea, there continued to be even more heated debates over key theological issues. What once seemed to be clear and unambiguous affirmations about Christ and God came to be challenged, reconsidered, modified, and made more specific and nuanced.

  o   As just one example, in the mid-4th century, the orthodox theologian Marcellus of Ancyra tried to understand how God can be "one" if he is Father, Son, and Holy Spirit.

  o   Marcellus's solution was that Christ and the Spirit were, in fact, coeternal with God, but prior to their appearance for the salvation of the world, they had been resident within God as part of him.

  o   Moreover, at the end of time, when salvation is complete, Christ and the Spirit will return inside God, without a separate existence for all eternity. In other words, the kingdom of Christ will come to an end; Christ will hand the kingdom over to God, and the Father will become all in all.

  o   This view was rejected by other orthodox thinkers, who considered it to be too much like modalism, in which the Father, Son, and Spirit were all the same person. Thus, Marcellus's view was declared a heresy, and a line was added to the Nicene Creed to note that Christ's kingdom "shall have no end."

- As a second and final example, we might consider the views of Apollinaris, who was consumed with the question of how Jesus Christ could be human and divine at the same time without being two things instead of one thing.

  o Apollinaris solved the problem by pointing out that humans are made up of three constituent parts: the body; the "lower soul," which is the root of our emotions and passions; and the "upper soul," which is the root of our faculty of reason.

  o Apollinaris maintained that in Jesus Christ, the Word of God, the *Logos*, replaced the upper soul; thus, Christ had God's reason within him, even though he was fully and truly a human body full of human emotions.

  o This view was condemned because it suggested that Christ was not really fully human because he lacked the upper soul or the spirit of a human. That would mean that we as full humans cannot imitate Christ's life and example because he was not really like one of us. It also meant that Christ could not redeem the entire human being because he was not himself fully human.

  o As a result, this view, too, came to be condemned as a heresy, and Christian theologians began to insist that Christ was not partly God and partly man; he was fully God and fully man at one and the same time.

Changing Understandings of Christ

- When we come to the theological disputes of the 4th century, it is clear that we are in an entirely different universe from the world of the historical Jesus and his followers.

- Jesus was a Jewish preacher of the coming apocalypse, who anticipated that the Son of Man—someone other than himself—

was soon to appear from heaven to destroy the forces of evil and set up God's good kingdom on earth. This was to happen soon, within his disciples' lifetimes.

- By the 4th century, Jesus was no longer a Jewish apocalyptic preacher of the imminent end. He was God Almighty, of the same substance with the Father, the one who created the universe, one who was eternally with the Father, and one who, with the Father and the Spirit, made up the divine Trinity that had always existed and would always exist as the one God over all.

- The Christian religion came to be predicated on this view of Christ.
    o It all started with the disciples' belief that Jesus had been raised from the dead. That made them think God had made him into a divine being.

    o Eventually, Jesus's followers thought he had been made divine not from the time of his Resurrection but from the time of his baptism. Soon, they maintained that he had been divine his entire life because God had made his virgin mother pregnant. Not long after that, they maintained that Jesus had existed before his birth as an angelic being who had temporarily become human.

    o Then, his followers began to say that Jesus was greater than an angel, greater even than the chief angel, that he was a subordinate divine being who had been created before all other things in the natural and supernatural worlds.

    o Finally, the followers of Jesus declared that he was fully and completely God, of the same essence as God the Father, equal with him in every way, eternal with him from before the beginning and until after the end, and a member of the blessed Trinity comprising Father, Son, and Spirit in a holy unity that never had and never would be broken.

- This Christ God who emerged in the 4th century is obviously a far cry from Jesus of Nazareth, who was crucified for crimes against the state. But it was this Christ God who conquered the Roman Empire and who continues to be the object of faith for billions of people in our world today.

Disciples believed that Jesus was raised from the dead.

God had made Jesus into a divine being.

Jesus was divine from the time of his baptism.

Jesus was divine his entire life.

Jesus had existed before his birth as an angelic being.

Jesus was greater than an angel, a subordinate divine being to God.

Jesus was fully and completely God.

Over the centuries, Christian belief progressed from the disciples' belief that Jesus had been raised from the dead to an understanding of Jesus as fully and completely God.

Suggested Reading

Carroll, *Constantine's Sword.*

Ehrman, *How Jesus Became God: The Exaltation of a Jewish Preacher from Galilee.*

Eusebius, *The History of the Church.*

Gager, *The Origin of Anti-Semitism.*

Harnack, *History of Dogma.*

Kelly, *Early Christian Doctrines.*

Osborn, *The Emergence of Christian Theology.*

Pelikan, *The Christian Tradition.*

Ruether, *Faith and Fratricide.*

Rusch, *The Trinitarian Controversy.*

Simon, *Verus Israel.*

Questions to Consider

1. How did the declaration that Jesus is fully God come to affect the relationships between Christians and Jews?

2. What kinds of debates over Christ and the Trinity continued after the decisions of the Council of Nicea?

Bibliography

Allison, Dale. *Jesus of Nazareth: Millenarian Prophet*. Minneapolis: Fortress Press, 1998. An authoritative but readable account of the historical Jesus that explains his life and teachings in light of his apocalyptic worldview.

————. *Resurrecting Jesus: The Earliest Christian Tradition and Its Interpreters*. New York: T&T Clark, 2005. Chapter 6 of this collection of essays gives a highly insightful discussion of the historical problems surrounding the Resurrection, written by one who nonetheless believes in it.

Bauer, Walter. *Orthodoxy and Heresy in Earliest Christianity*. Philadelphia: Fortress Press, 1971. One of the most important books of the 20th century on the history of early Christianity. Bauer argues against the classical understanding of orthodoxy and heresy by maintaining that what was later called heresy was, in many regions of early Christendom, the oldest and most prominent form of Christian belief.

Bentall, Richard P. "Hallucinatory Experiences." In *Varieties of Anomalous Experience: Examining the Scientific Evidence*, edited by Etzel Cardeña, et al. Washington DC: American Psychological Association, 2000. A modern psychologist shows the frequency of hallucinatory experiences and explains their psychological basis.

Brakke, David. *The Gnostics: Myth, Ritual and Diversity in Early Christianity*. Cambridge, MA: Harvard University Press, 2010. The best recent book on early Christian Gnosticism.

Brown, Raymond. *The Death of the Messiah: From Gethsemane to the Grave*. 2 vols. London: Doubleday, 1994. A detailed and thorough discussion of the Passion narratives of the four Gospels in all of their aspects and for all of their verses.

————. *An Introduction to the New Testament*. New York: Doubleday, 1997. A full and authoritative introduction to all of the major issues pertaining to the study of the New Testament by one of the premier New Testament scholars of the second half of the 20th century. It includes extensive and up-to-date bibliographies.

————. *The Virginal Conception and Bodily Resurrection of Jesus.* Mahwah, NJ: Paulist Press, 1972. An authoritative but accessible discussion of Jesus's alleged miraculous birth and Resurrection, from literary, theological, and historical perspectives, by an important Roman Catholic scholar of the New Testament.

Carroll, John. *Constantine's Sword: The Church and the Jews, A History.* Boston: Houghton Mifflin, 2001. A terrific and widely popular account of Jewish-Christian relations, beginning with Jesus and moving to the modern period but focusing on the significance of Constantine's conversion for understanding the history of anti-Judaism in Western civilization.

Cartlidge, David R., and David L. Dungan, eds. *Documents for the Study of the Gospels.* 2nd ed. Philadelphia: Fortress Press, 1994. Presents a valuable selection of ancient literary texts that have close parallels to the New Testament Gospels, including portions of Philostratus's *Life of Apollonius*.

Casey, Maurice. *From Jewish Prophet to Gentile God: The Origins and Development of New Testament Christology.* Louisville, KY: Westminster John Knox, 1991. A controversial explanation of how Jesus came to be seen no longer as a Jewish preacher but as a divine being.

Collins, Adela Yarbro, and John J. Collins. *King and Messiah as Son of God: Divine, Human, and Angelic Messianic Figures in Biblical and Related Literature.* Grand Rapids, MI: Eerdmans, 2008. An excellent collection of essays dealing with different understandings of the messiah in early Judaism.

Collins, John. *The Apocalyptic Imagination: An Introduction to the Matrix of Christianity.* New York: Crossroad, 1984. A fine treatment of Jewish apocalypticism as the context for the proclamation of Jesus and his followers.

————. *The Star and Scepter: Messianism in Light of the Dead Sea Scrolls.* 2nd ed. Grand Rapids, MI: Eerdmans, 2010. An up-to-date discussion of Jewish messianic expectation around the time of Jesus.

Connell, Janice T. *Meetings with Mary: Visions of the Blessed Mother.* New York: Ballantine Books, 1995. An anecdotal account of the various appearances of Mary, the mother of Jesus, in visions to her devotees.

Dunn, James D. G. *Christology in the Making: A New Testament Inquiry into the Origins of the Doctrine of the Incarnation.* 2nd ed. Grand Rapids, MI: Eerdmans, 1989. A standard and now-classic description of the development of early Christology in the New Testament period.

Dünzel, Franz. *A Brief History of the Doctrine of the Trinity in the Early Church.* John Bowden, trans. London: T&T Clark, 2007. An accessible and insightful study of the development of the Christian doctrine of the Trinity.

Ehrman, Bart. *How Jesus Became God: The Exaltation of a Jewish Preacher from Galilee.* San Francisco: HarperOne, 2014.

————. *Lost Christianities: The Battles for Scripture and the Faiths We Never Knew.* New York: Oxford University Press, 2003. A study of the wide-ranging diversity of Christianity in the 2nd and 3rd centuries, of the sacred texts (many of them forged) produced and revered by different Christian groups of the period, and of the struggles that led to the emergence of "orthodox" Christianity prior to the conversion of Constantine.

————. *Jesus: Apocalyptic Prophet of the New Millennium.* New York, Oxford University Press, 1999. Written by the instructor of the course, this study considers all the evidence for the historical Jesus, including recent archaeological discoveries and noncanonical sources, and argues that he is best understood as an apocalyptic prophet who expected God soon to intervene in the course of history to overthrow the forces of evil and bring in his good kingdom.

Eusebius. *The History of the Church*. G. A. Williamson, ed. and trans. London: Penguin, 1965. A terrific translation of the 4th-century Eusebius's indispensable chronicle of the first three centuries of Christianity.

Fitzmyer, Joseph. *Pauline Theology: A Brief Sketch*. 2nd ed. Englewood Cliffs, NJ: Prentice Hall, 1989. A brief but superb overview of the major aspects of Paul's theological views.

Fredriksen, Paula. *From Jesus to Christ: The Origins of the New Testament Images of Christ*. 2nd ed. New Haven: Yale University Press, 2000. An important study of the earliest Christian views of Jesus and of the ways they developed as Christianity moved away from its Jewish roots.

————. *Jesus of Nazareth, King of the Jews: A Jewish Life and the Emergence of Christianity*. New York: Knopf, 1999. A lively sketch of the life and teachings of Jesus that takes seriously the Jewish world in which he lived and pays close attention to the problems posed by our surviving sources.

Friesen, Steven J. *Imperial Cults and the Apocalypse of John: Reading Revelation in the Ruins*. New York: Oxford University Press, 2001. A study of the worship of the emperor in the Roman Empire, especially as it relates to the book of Revelation.

Gager, John. *The Origin of Anti-Semitism: Attitudes toward Judaism in Pagan and Christian Antiquity*. New York: Oxford University Press, 1983. A now-classic study of the relationship of Jews with non-Jews in antiquity.

Garrett, Susan R. *No Ordinary Angel: Celestial Spirits and Christian Claims about Jesus*. New Haven: Yale University Press, 2008. An extremely useful study of early Christian understandings of Jesus as an angel.

Gieschen, Charles A. *Angelomorphic Christology: Antecedents and Early Evidence*. Leiden: Brill, 1998. A highly scholarly assessment of early Christian views of Christ as an angel.

155

Goulder, Michael. "The Baseless Fabric of a Vision." In *Resurrection Reconsidered*, edited by Gavin D'Costa, pp. 48–61. Oxford: One World Press, 1996. A controversial discussion of Jesus's Resurrection that denies its historical reality.

Grant, Robert M. *Jesus after the Gospels: The Christ of the Second Century*. Louisville, KY: Westminster John Knox, 1990. An intriguing discussion of different understandings of Christology in the decades after the New Testament was written, among a variety of early Christian groups.

Groh, Dennis, and Robert Gregg. *Early Arianism: A View of Salvation*. Philadelphia: Fortress Press, 1981. A classical study of the views of Arius and his followers.

Guggenheim, Bill, and Judy Guggenheim. *Hello from Heaven! A New Field of Research—After-Death Communications—Confirms That Life and Love Are Eternal*. New York: Bantam Books, 1995. A popular and anecdotal account of visions experienced by people of their departed loved ones.

Harnack, Adolf von. *History of Dogma*. Vol. 1. Neil Buchanan, trans. (3rd ed.). New York: Dover, 1961 (German original, 1900). A classic and invaluable sketch of the development of Christian theology during the early centuries of the church, by one of the most erudite historians of Christianity of modern times.

———. *Marcion: The Gospel of the Alien God*. Durham, NC: Labyrinth, 1990. This is the classic study, published in German in 1924, of the life and teachings of the 2nd-century Christian theologian Marcion.

Hengel, Martin. *Between Jesus and Paul: Studies in the History of Earliest Christianity*. London: SCM Press, 1983. A collection of essays on important aspects of the development of Christian thought during its earliest years, prior to the writing of the books of the New Testament.

———. *The Son of God: The Origin of Christology and the History of Jewish-Hellenistic Religion*. Philadelphia: Fortress Press, 1976 (German original, 1975). A study of the rise of Christology and the relationship of claims of Jesus to understandings of the divine world in other religions at the time.

Hurtado, Larry W. *Lord Jesus Christ: Devotion to Jesus in Earliest Christianity*. Grand Rapids, MI: Eerdmans, 2003. A full, detailed, and scholarly study of how the Christians, from the earliest of times, worshipped Christ as God.

————. *One God, One Lord: Early Christian Devotion and Ancient Jewish Monotheism*. London: SCM Press, 1988. A valuable study that argues that the source of conflict between early Christians and nonChristian Jews was not, strictly speaking, over whether Jesus could be thought of as divine but whether he was worshipped.

Kelly, J. N. D. *Early Christian Doctrines*. 2nd ed. San Francisco: Harper One, 1978. A historical survey of the development of such fundamental Christian doctrines as those involving Christ and the Trinity.

King, Karen. *What Is Gnosticism?* Cambridge, MA: Harvard University Press, 2005. Here, a prominent scholar of Gnosticism asks whether it is appropriate to use the category of Gnosticism any longer.

Kysar, Robert. *John the Maverick Gospel*. Atlanta: John Knox, 1976. This is one of the best introductions to the distinctive features of John's Gospel; pays particular attention to how John differs from the Synoptics in many of its major perspectives on Jesus.

Lane Fox, Robin. *Pagans and Christians*. New York: Alfred A. Knopf, 1987. A long but fascinating discussion of the relationship of pagans and Christians during the first centuries of Christianity, valuable especially for its brilliant sketch of what it meant to be a "pagan" in the 2nd and 3rd centuries C.E.

Laurentin, René. *The Apparitions of the Blessed Virgin Mary Today*. Dublin: Veritas, 1990 (French original, 1988). A popular account of visions of Jesus's mother, Mary, in the modern world, by a highly educated believer in these visions.

Layton, Bentley. *The Gnostic Scriptures: A New Translation with Annotations*. Garden City, NY: Doubleday, 1987. An invaluable translation of important Gnostic documents, including those discovered at Nag Hammadi and those quoted by the church fathers, with a useful introductory sketch on Gnosticism.

Lüdemann, Gerd. *The Resurrection of Christ: A Historical Inquiry*. Amherst, NY: Prometheus Books, 2004. A controversial book by a controversial German biblical scholar who casts doubt on the historicity of Jesus's Resurrection.

Meier, John. *A Marginal Jew: Rethinking the Historical Jesus*. 4 vols. New York: Doubleday, 1991–2009. The first of four volumes on the historical Jesus, this is an authoritative account that covers the sources available for the study of Jesus's birth and the questions surrounding it.

Norris, Richard. *The Christological Controversy*. Philadelphia: Fortress Press, 1980. A useful presentation of some of the major texts from antiquity involving the controversies over the nature and person of Christ.

Osborn, Eric. *The Emergence of Christian Theology*. New York: Cambridge University Press, 1993. A standard study of the development of early Christian doctrines, including those of Christ.

Pelikan, Jeroslav. *The Christian Tradition*. Vol. 1. Chicago: University of Chicago Press, 1971. An authoritative discussion of the theology of early Christians in the first centuries of the church.

Peppard, Michael. *The Son of God in the Roman World: Divine Sonship in Its Social and Political Context*. New York: Oxford University Press, 2011. An impressive scholarly discussion of what it meant in the Roman world for a person to be "adopted" as a son, as Jesus was thought to be adopted to be the Son of God.

Price, S. R. F. *Rituals and Power: The Roman Imperial Cult in Asia Minor*. New York: Cambridge University Press, 1984. A classic and authoritative study of the emperor cult in a major portion of the Roman Empire.

Bibliography

Rives, James. *Religion in the Roman Empire*. Malden, MA: Wiley-Blackwell, 2006. This is the best introduction available at a popular level to the "pagan" religions in the Roman world.

Ruether, Rosemary. *Faith and Fratricide: The Theological Roots of Anti-Semitism*. New York: Seabury, 1974. A controversial discussion of the early Christian attitudes toward Jews and Judaism, which maintains that anti-Semitism is the necessary corollary of Christian belief in Jesus as the messiah.

Rusch, William G. *The Trinitarian Controversy*. Philadelphia: Fortress Press, 1980. A valuable collection of ancient Christian writers who discuss the doctrine of the Trinity, with clear and sensible introductions.

Sanders, E. P. *The Historical Figure of Jesus*. London: Penguin, 1993. One of the best available introductions to the life and teachings of the historical Jesus. It is well-suited for beginning students.

———. *Judaism Practice and Belief, 63 BCE–66 CE*. London and Philadelphia: SCM Press/Trinity Press International, 1992. A full, detailed, and authoritative account of what it meant to be a Jew immediately before and during the time of the New Testament, by one of the great New Testament scholars of our generation.

Schweitzer, Albert. *The Quest of the Historical Jesus*. New York: Macmillan, 1968. This is the classic study of the major attempts to write a biography of Jesus up to the first part of the 20th century. (The German original appeared in 1906.) It is also one of the first and perhaps the most important attempt to portray Jesus as a Jewish apocalypticist.

Segal, Alan. *Paul the Convert: The Apostolate and Apostasy of Saul the Pharisee*. New Haven: Yale University Press, 1990. An intriguing assessment of the teachings and theology of Paul in light of the Judaism of his day, focusing on the role and significance of his "conversion" to become a follower of Jesus; written by an important scholar of ancient Judaism.

————. *Two Powers in Heaven: Early Rabbinic Reports about Christianity and Gnosticism*. Leiden: Brill, 1977. An important scholarly account of early Jewish traditions that there was a second divine being accompanying God in heaven as a model for what Christians claimed about Jesus.

Simon, Marcel. *Verus Israel: A Study of the Relations between Christians and Jews in the Roman Empire (135–425)*. H. McKeating, trans. Oxford: Oxford University Press, 1986. A standard study of Jewish-Christian relations in the early centuries of the church.

Smith, D. Moody. *The Theology of John*. New York: Cambridge University Press, 1994. A clearly written and incisive discussion of the major themes of John by one of the premier scholars of the fourth Gospel.

Tobin, Thomas H. "Logos." In *The Anchor Bible Dictionary*, edited by David Noel Friedman, vol. 4, pp. 348–356. New York: Doubleday, 1999. A useful article that explains how *Logos* (the "Word") was understood both in Greek and Roman circles (for example, Stoicism) and in Jewish circles. A useful guide for how Christians understood Christ to be the Word of God (as in John 1).

Turcan, Robert. *The Cults of the Roman Empire*. Oxford: Blackwell, 1996. A superb introduction to some of the major religious cults in the Roman Empire from roughly the time of early Christianity (and before).

Vermes, Geza. *Jesus the Jew: A Historian's Reading of the Gospels*. New York: Macmillan, 1973. A readable but very learned study of Jesus in light of traditions of other Jewish "holy men" from his time, written by a prominent New Testament scholar at Oxford.

Wiebe, Phillip H. *Visions of Jesus: Direct Encounters from the New Testament to Today*. New York: Oxford University Press, 1997. A fascinating discussion of appearances of Jesus in visions of Christian believers today.

Bibliography